MarketPlace	: AUK
Order Number	: 202-6917489-4681926
Ship Method	: Standard
Order Date	: 2015-03-24
Email	: txh8zjblbwp7bc6@marketplace.amazon.co.uk

Items : 1

Qty	Item	Locator
1	Improving Teaching and Learning in the Arts (Looki	HOL-3-UH-117-03-15
	ISBN : 0750707992	OD

RCode: ||| |||||||||||||||||||| ||||||||||||||||||||||| ||||| |||||||||||||||||| ||||| ||| ||| |||| ||| || |||

Mulberry House, Woods Way, Goring By Sea, West Sussex, BN12 4QY. Tel:+44(0)1903 507544
Email: sales@worldofbooks.com | Twitter: @WorldofBooksltd | Web: www.worldofbooks.com

Improving teaching and learning in the arts

Edited by Mary Kear and Gloria Callaway

FALMER PRESS
Taylor & Francis Group

First published 2000 by Falmer Press
11 New Fetter Lane, London EC4P 4EE

Simultaneously published in the USA and Canada
by Falmer Press
19 Union Square West, New York, NY 10003

Falmer Press is an imprint of the Taylor & Francis Group

Typeset in Melior by Graphicraft Limited, Hong Kong
Printed and bound in Great Britain by TJ International Ltd,
Padstow, Cornwall

British Library Cataloguing in Publication Data
A catalogue record for this book is available from the British Library

Library of Congress Cataloging in Publication Data
Improving teaching and learning in the arts / edited by Mary Kear and
     Gloria Callaway.
          p.   cm. — (Looking afresh at the primary curriculum)
     Includes bibliographical references and index.
     1. Arts—Study and teaching (Elementary)—Great Britain.
I. Kear, Mary.   II. Callaway, Gloria.   III. Series.
LB1591.5.G7I56   2000   99–36832
372.5′044′0941—dc21

Cover design by Carla Turchini

ISBN 0 7507 0799 2

Contents

Part III
Celebrating the arts for everyone

Series editors' preface
Kate Ashcroft and David James

Improving teaching and learning in the arts is one of a series of books in the Looking Afresh at the Primary Curriculum Series edited by Kate Ashcroft and David James. Other books in the series include:

    Improving teaching and learning in the core curriculum, edited by Kate Ashcroft and John Lee; and

    Improving teaching and learning in the humanities, edited by Martin Ashley.

Like the other books in the series, *Improving teaching and learning in the arts* is written as an essential support for students training for primary teaching in colleges and universities, those undertaking inservice teacher education and teachers in schools wishing to use an accessible text to get in touch with some of the more recent thinking about the primary curriculum. It is a natural 'next step' from the two introductory texts published by Falmer Press, that cover the whole curriculum:

    The Primary Teacher's Guide to the New National Curriculum, edited by Kate Ashcroft and David Palacio; and

    Implementing the Primary Curriculum, edited by Kate Ashcroft and David Palacio.

The present series is intended to build on and further develop knowledge about the curriculum that was included at an introductory level in the two books above and in particular asks the reader to look in more depth at the link between the arts and children's learning in schools. It is aimed at supporting students and teachers who are beginning to get to grips with what it means to be a curriculum specialist for one of the National Curriculum subjects in a primary school.

The book could be used in various ways. It will be of use for teachers and student teachers wishing to gain an overview of aspects of teacher education programmes related to the arts curriculum. It is also designed to be used by student teachers at the stage when they are beginning that part of their course that applies to the role of an arts specialist in the primary school. The enquiry-based format provides a starting point for the sort of enquiry, reflection and learning that tutors are trying to encourage within initial teacher education and inservice courses based on the Reflective Teacher Model.

The books in the series are well signposted with headings and subheadings, with lots of practical suggestions of ways of going about curriculum planning, reflection and enquiry. There is some reference to theory, but wherever possible, this is illustrated with practical examples in the form of case studies that highlight implications for the enquiring teacher.

The series does not aim to present outcomes of research to be absorbed by teachers, nor does it focus on their skills as educational researchers *per se*; nor does it attempt to give a list of tips. It is focused on enquiry with a view to improving practice through:

- accessible content at the reader's level about the main issues;
- knowledge about a range of teaching methods and curriculum content;
- knowledge about the way information and communicative technologies can influence teaching, learning and curriculum content;
- enquiry tasks that encourage the reader to:
  - assess and develop their understandings of the issues
  - assess and develop their subject knowledge
  - try out activities in the classroom and collect data about their effects and effectiveness;
- an annotated reading list at the end of each chapter.

Although some of the ideas contained in the series are complex and could be seen as demanding, the authors have been careful to keep the style of the books straightforward and the language is accessible rather than 'academic'. Wherever possible, new ideas and concepts are supported by concrete examples. The authors' intention is to communicate clearly some of the complexity and subtlety of effective and reflective teaching.

The chapters within the book are linked by common themes: the principles of the Reflective Practitioner Model are an essential element. These are outlined in some detail in Ashcroft and Palacio (1995 and 1997). These principles include the need to look at issues of equality. Inclusivity and the dilemmas raised for the reflective teacher working within a largely constrained curriculum context are important foci for discussion.

The chapters raise the problematic nature of much of our 'taken for granted' knowledge about the curriculum. They look at intended as well as unintended consequences of action and the need for teachers to constantly remain openminded and responsible. Openmindedness implies that the reader neither rejects nor accepts the accepted orthodoxies about teaching and curriculum, but rather seeks to test ideas against the reality of their classroom and the available and emerging research and other evidence. The authors stress that this is not an objective and value-free process. The reader will be confronted with issues of responsibility: the need to consider ethical issues and the long-term as well as the immediate consequences of action. In particular, readers will be asked to look beyond a utilitarian stance, beyond 'what works', in order to look at the role of values in teaching and learning.

The authors present a view of reflective practice as an evaluation-led activity, that requires the collection of evidence about teaching, learning, assessment, values, beliefs and behaviour. This analysis is located within a moral, spiritual, social and cultural context. The meanings and experience of the various parties to the educational process are carefully considered.

The book also deals with the more immediate challenges that confront teachers in today's classrooms, including information and communicative technologies: their use and the issues they raise. In dealing with these issues the stress is on creativity in teaching and learning and the ways that such creativity can illuminate possibilities and problems such as those of match, progression and differentiation in teaching and learning. Throughout the focus is on the analysis of effective teaching and learning. Understanding effectiveness requires an exploration of meanings underpinning current debates (for example, notions such as 'basics' and 'standards'). In this discussion, the book also addresses the political agenda in which the teaching of the arts takes place.

A reflective approach to these issues leads to a focus on dilemmas rather than simple answers. This can be frustrating for new teachers looking for simple prescriptions for the problems that they face. We hope that the use of case study material describing the ways that real-life teachers have tackled some of these dilemmas, their successes and failures, will help to bring the issues alive. Although there can be few 'tips', the inclusion of knowledge-base for action, together with suggested sources for extending knowledge-base beyond that possible within the scope of the book should leave the reader in a position to make better and more informed decisions within their particular context. Such decisions are always context specific: there are many simple educational questions, but we are increasingly certain that there are no simple answers. For this reason, authors have tried to locate the content and tasks within a theoretical framework. This framework is essential to inform action and decision-making in a range of contexts.

References

ASHCROFT, K. and LEE, J. (eds) (1999) *Improving teaching and learning in the core curriculum*, London: Falmer Press.

ASHCROFT, K. and PALACIO, D. (eds) (1995) *The Primary Teacher's Guide to the New National Curriculum*, London: Falmer Press.

ASHCROFT, K. and PALACIO, D. (eds) (1997) *Implementing the Primary Curriculum*, London: Falmer Press.

ASHLEY, M. (ed.) (1999) *Improving teaching and learning in the humanities*, London: Falmer Press.

Part I   Common issues

Introduction: developing primary practice in the arts
Gloria Callaway

Teaching and learning in the arts

Teaching has been described as a vocation, a profession and other things besides, but most often as an art. As reflective teachers, we learn more about children as we teach them; as they learn, we learn. We also learn about teaching by watching more skilled practitioners in action, and by studying useful theory arrived at by experts in the field. Observation, study and reflection on our own and others' practice helps all of us to improve, if we allow the expertise of more skilled others to inform our work, and if we learn in equal measure from our successes and failures.

This is particularly true of teaching in, through and about the arts. Adults as well as children learn about the arts from looking at, watching and listening to skilled artists or artistes; from being taught by more able teachers, and, of course, from their peers. This often involves practical engagement, trying out ideas, and attempting to relate this personal experience to knowledge and understanding gained from other sources.

The term 'art' is listed, in the *Collins Thesaurus* (1995) along with the words *craft, skill, mastery, expertise* and *knowledge*, all of which carry with them the notion of something that can be taught, passed on, perhaps in an apprenticeship model. But we also get the words *aptitude, knack* and *virtuosity*, which might imply that the arts are a gift, which we either have or don't have: something over which we have little control. This is a widely held belief, one which we intend to challenge during the course of this book.

While there is undoubtedly a range of skills and aptitudes evident in any group of children, there is every reason to assume that the arts *can* be taught. Equally, there is every reason to assume that we support children's creativity by well structured teaching, offering appropriate models and examples of artists' and artistes' work, and encouraging the best practice in every sense.

Teaching and learning in the arts is rightly considered as beneficial across the curriculum, although we do not propose that we teach the arts because they help children do better at mathematics. (Try to reverse that statement, and see how it reads.) Learning in and through the arts complements and supports achievement, it promotes clear thinking, logical decision-making and considered approaches to problem-solving.

> *Just because artistic judgements are not open to scientific verification, it does not follow that they are closed to all forms of verification. There are different kinds of reasoning. . . . feeling and reason need not be considered dichotomous; it is the interplay between them which leads to a more comprehensive form of knowledge. Thus, to deny students access to the arts is to deny them access to a more comprehensible, richer, way of knowing than is possible within the limitations of 'scientific rationality'.* (Bergman, 1993, pp. 109–12)

We argue here that a comprehensive arts education within the primary curriculum is vital, both for its intrinsic worth, and as a necessary complement to other aspects of learning. Through experiences in the arts, children learn, for instance, to interpret illustrations and pictures of objects and creatures they have never encountered in 'real life', such as dinosaurs and the cities of ancient civilisations, beanstalks that grow to enormous heights and machines that travel through time and space. Like adults, they build on their own experience of the world around them, to access the imaginary worlds of others, and to make their own. 'Imagination' is based on personal experiences and the ability to imbue known phenomena with wondrous and unknown qualities. This is surely both a function and the product of a worthwhile arts education.

Primary teachers and the arts

In primary schools, teaching the arts poses particular problems for some teachers, because of uncertainty about their own skills and knowledge, and even from a feeling of guilt about spending time which they feel should be devoted to core subjects. Yet there can be few teachers who are not familiar with many different forms of music, visual arts and drama. Cameras and computers are part of our everyday lives, as are newspapers, televisions and other media technologies. When we teach children, we try to start with what they know. So it may be helpful for us to acknowledge the vast wealth of knowledge and understandings *we* have, and to use it as a basis for teaching others.

This lack of confidence, lack of resources or limited space have been cited as reasons for the low status often afforded to teaching the arts in some schools. Perhaps such factors also contribute to a focus on 'doing' rather than 'learning'. When time is perceived as being limited, the tendency has been to cut corners on the *process*, in order to achieve *products*. Throughout this book are examples of children and teachers creating 'products'. However, we want to stress that the arts are primarily concerned with complex thought-processing, and so they make significant contributions to the development of children's thinking skills. That is how good 'products' evolve.

 Effective art teaching will support and encourage development of personal vision and therefore demand independence of thought from the student.

(Ross, 1985, p. 78)

Such independence can be challenging for teachers, who may find it hard to strike an appropriate balance between expressive action and structured learning. The arts can be noisy, messy and profligate consumers of time, space and resources. But primary teachers are skilled organisers, competent managers and able to make amazing silk purses from the most unpromising of sows' ears. The aim of this book is to support the reader in building on existing skills and understandings. Through case studies, starting points for reflection and specific enquiry tasks, we suggest how to develop theoretical perspectives through careful consideration of issues which influence everyday practice.

Chapter 1, therefore, examines four major issues, which we believe are central to the debate about the role and function of arts education today. They are concerned with: a definition of 'arts'; the relationship between 'making' (practical activity) and 'consuming' (experiencing and appreciating) in the arts; the pros and cons of 'combined' and 'discrete' arts provision, and the existence (or not) of a common 'artistic process' which informs making in all main art forms.

The role of the arts in the primary school

An important consideration, which underpins all our work in primary school, is how we, as teachers, position children as learners within the arts curriculum. The notion that children are mini-artists and performers is a tempting one. We certainly encourage them to display and make visual, musical and dramatic products for their peers and others to enjoy. But this is only one aspect of the arts in primary schools; not all artistic endeavours in the classroom are for public consumption. Think about role play, creative writing, personal sketchbook use and other creative pursuits which may serve as an end in themselves, for the pleasure of the participant or participants alone. Music making is surely not only and solely as rehearsal for performance: improvisation, composition and singing can happen unobserved, unheard, by anyone but the player or singer.

On the other hand, where a performance or exhibition is the intended outcome, skills already learned and practised are drawn on, and developed as appropriate for the 'public event'. In schools, such events can be appreciated at different levels. Highly accomplished, technically competent and skilfully staged work is always a joy for the audience, be it the class assembly or the prestigious school concert. Children understand and appreciate the formal conventions which apply in such situations, and are able to rise to the occasion.

There is, increasingly in our experience, a worrying tendency to make the formal performance or exhibition the *rationale* for teaching in the arts, for example, when all singing or dance activities are geared towards a production, or when artwork gets frenetically generated to decorate walls in order to impress inspectors or parents of potential students. In itself, this is understandable, given today's pressures on time, space and energies, but we need to ask whether this is sufficient to equip children with the breadth of experience that comes from a different pedagogical focus.

In planning and implementing classroom-based arts education (that is, not including special clubs or other extra-curricular activities), it has become increasingly important to ensure that our aims and purposes are very clear. There is a (legal) obligation to provide a broad and balanced curriculum, in which the integral role of the arts is acknowledged, and resourced accordingly. Therefore, the public event, so vital to the life of a school, its pupils and its community, is perhaps better seen as a *culmination* and celebration of creative, well structured teaching and learning, rather than as its *raison d'être.* It is, ideally, part and parcel of the term's or year's teaching, not an add-on 'extra', an additional burden on top of the 'normal' work of the class.

Case studies in Chapters 1, 2 and 8 provide a range of examples where an appropriate balance is effected between 'process' and 'product', in arts education. Chapter 2, for instance, describes and discusses the role of narrative in the arts, focusing on how the story acts as a unifying theme across art forms, promoting knowledge and understanding, and giving status and value to dramatic performance.

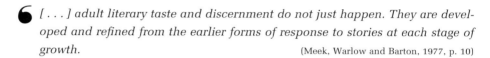

[. . .] adult literary taste and discernment do not just happen. They are developed and refined from the earlier forms of response to stories at each stage of growth. (Meek, Warlow and Barton, 1977, p. 10)

Chapter 8 explores further the significance of public events in school, with exemplars of how skills and techniques taught as part of the whole curriculum are brought together to celebrate achievement in and through the arts.

Children in control?

The chapters in the second section of the book deal with particular art forms, and each develops ideas set out in Chapter 1. Chapters 3 and 4 explore issues related to links between the 'maker' and 'consumer' roles adopted by us and the children we teach. Talking with children about art and music is an area of uncertainty for most of us. How the work of adult practitioners influences child learners has been too little explored to date: it was over two decades ago that we were first alerted to the tensions between 'copying' and 'modelling', in the realm of children's literature.

We see characters and events from books reappearing in children's play, in their writing, and in what at first sight look like 'original' stories made up by children. We know very little about obvious obstacles – how children understand narrated time sequences, or the eliptical structure of a ballad or narrative poem. What clues do they follow to construe a narrative, other than the 'rule of three' for the fairy-story, for example? (Meek, Warlow and Barton, 1977, p. 9)

The apprentice writer has much in common with the apprentice artist, musician or dancer. Children have the capacity to take on board, and make their own use of, models of good practice offered and mediated by a more knowledgeable other, usually an adult, most often a teacher.

Modelling is a healthy and creative way of working in the arts, recognising useful elements and techniques used by others, and putting them together with imagination to produce an original and expressive work. In contrast, encouraging direct 'copying' or the use of adult-generated 'templates' implies that children are incapable of achieving an acceptable standard, and denies them ultimate ownership of their own work. Such an approach demonstrates a lack of trust in the children's abilities, and breeds a lack of self-confidence.

In their day-to-day work, teachers are able to position themselves as directors, producers and controllers of children's creative endeavours. Alternatively, working in a more democratically inspired mode, they can empower children to take on these roles for themselves, and to develop skills which enable them to have ownership of their work. Chapter 6 describes an approach to classroom learning in communications technology, where children examine and analyse media products made by adults, and use the information and understanding they gain to manipulate words, images, sounds and music to express and communicate their own ideas.

Arts products as cultural artefacts

In primary schools, we pride ourselves on offering children a range of experiences, a wide cultural and inter-cultural diet which will broaden horizons, and make available to them ideas, images and phenomena they might otherwise not encounter. The models teachers offer their pupils, including those vicariously experienced, for example via television or other media, are the products of their cultural environments. In Chapter 5, dance tuition for a specific event (carnival) describes effective interplay between teachers, dancers, children and their families, where the school provides a catalyst for promoting 'cultural understanding'.

'Culture' has been variously described, notably by Edward Taylor in 1871 as:

❛ *[. . .] that complex whole which includes knowledge, belief, art, morals, law, custom, and many other capabilities acquired by man as a member of society.*

(cited in Ross, 1985, p. 6)

Culture comprises much more than the arts, although Ross (1985, p. 13) argues that 'artistic practice is an indispensable tool for heightening and transforming consciousness'. Cultural experience can help people to feel and think in new ways. Its inclusion in the curriculum has been justified partly in terms of its contribution to:

– *developing skills, problem-solving, developing the imagination and creativity (or)*
 – *awareness, understanding, development of feeling.* (Meeson, 1985, p. 55)

Children and their teachers bring to school their own rich, diverse and unique histories of looking at art and artefacts, listening to a range of music and experiencing drama in many forms. Some may be, on the surface, 'common' experiences, but even if we have all been in the same place at the same time, our responses will be individual and unique, and we must respect the right of others to respond in a way different from our own.

Imagine the following artists sitting together to paint a scene: O'Keeffe, Matisse, Michelangelo, Hockney, Riley and Rembrandt. Although each artist works or worked within what can be termed a 'Western' tradition, each would have highly personal responses to the scene, and each painting would be unique and individual.

The challenging nature of the arts

When we discuss the arts with children, such as music, sculpture or a dance performance, we sometimes fail to acknowledge our personal, possibly best unvoiced, response to the experience, and stay in the comfortable and non-threatening zone of description and retelling. But the arts often fulfil a deliberate function in making us uncomfortable, for instance, Dennis Potter's television drama, Damien Hirst's sculptures or (in its time) an Impressionist painting. Such paintings are often described now as having restful, tranquil properties, although the view of the art establishment when they were made was less than favourable. Will people in future grace their living-room walls with miniature plastic reproductions of Damien Hirst's animals in formaldehyde?

Whatever our backgrounds or level of understanding and knowledge within the field of the arts, there are very few in the world, let alone in the primary teaching profession, who can claim an understanding of the complete range we would like to introduce to the children we teach. It may be that we need to take more courage in daring to introduce ourselves and our pupils to, for example, works of art or pieces of music, which challenge us because they are unfamiliar or even unfathomable.

While we have a duty to acquaint children with a wide range of ideas, we need to avoid unnecessary 'them and us' divisions in effecting that mediation, while valuing the differences which exist within and between groups and peoples in our own communities and other cultural settings. We also owe it to our pupils to research, and to encourage them to research, to acquire information to inform our own responses, and to assist us in adopting the role of mediator. It can be dangerous to resort to simplistic explanations, which potentially contribute to a stereotypical view of the cultural environment in which the work is produced, thereby demeaning the work, the artists and the very cultural environment we attempt to describe.

Challenges in arts education feature strongly in Chapter 7, which considers how the arts provide a vehicle for learning, especially for pupils with special educational needs. It is particularly important for teachers working with such pupils, in mainstream or 'special' schools, to identify and acknowledge the potential within the arts to contribute, in many differing ways, to social and emotional development, communications skills and physical and cognitive development. What is not appropriate, within any art form or any school, is for the teacher to assume the role of a therapist.

> *It is appropriate here to state very firmly that therapy is a professional area on which primary teachers impinge not only at their own peril but, more import-antly, at severe risk of endangering the pupils they seek to help.*
>
> (Callaway and Kear, 1999, p. 111)

With all pupils, in all types of school, the arts provide an expressive outlet, and a learning tool. By their very nature, they invite participation and response, they inspire and challenge. In this, the arts are intrinsically 'inclusive', because every one of us has the ability to be involved in some way, at some level.

The complexity and sophistication of the primary teacher's daily work is often underestimated. It requires perception, imagination, knowledge and understanding of how children learn, about the subjects they are to learn and how best to communicate relevant ideas, information and concepts. Teachers orchestrate, choreograph, compose, design and construct the curriculum and the classroom ethos for their pupils.

This book aims to celebrate teaching and the arts in their many forms, which offer children a route to independent judgement, and opportunities to make valid individual and collaborative responses to experience. Its authors are passionately concerned with raising standards in all areas of teaching and learning, in promoting inclusivity through the arts, and in facilitating for children an appropriate degree of autonomy to enable them to express themselves confidently, and thereby communicate effectively.

 Arts are cognitive activities, guided by human intelligence, that make unique forms of meaning possible. (Eisner, 1985, p. 201)

References

BERGMAN, S. (1993) 'An epistemological justification for aesthetic experience', *Journal of Aesthetic Education* **27**(2), pp. 107–12.

CALLAWAY, G. and KEAR, M. (1999) *Teaching Art and Design in the Primary School,* London: David Fulton.

EISNER, E. (1985) *The Art of Educational Evaluation,* Sussex: Falmer Press.

MEEK, M., WARLOW, A. and BARTON, G. (1977) *The Cool Web: The Pattern of Children's Reading,* London: Bodley Head.

MEESON, P. (1985) 'Aestheticism and responsibility in art education', in ROSS, M. (1985).

ROSS, M. (ed.) (1985) *The Aesthetic in Education,* London: Pergamon.

Chapter 1

The arts in the primary school

Gloria Callaway and Mary Kear

Case Study I

The school entrance was decked with children's work about animals: drawings, paintings, sculptures, photographs, prints and fabrics, illustrated poems and stories, and scaled drawings to represent the relative sizes of giraffes, elephants, snails and goldfish. Posters announced next week's school concert, when each class would contribute an item of music, dance, recitation or drama. From the hall came grunts, screams, yells and laughter as children rehearsed their play. In the nearest classroom, children painted their imaginary animal puppets, edited poems on a word processor or huddled over a tape recorder. A group of seven-year-olds rehearsed using a video camera, to record the visit of the local vet. Some ten-year-olds practised singing their own updated version of 'Old Macdonald' to an original arrangement of the music by their classmates. An air of excitement and expectation heralded the climax of the summer term's 'arts focus', around the theme of 'animal magic'. This school did not suddenly blossom into an arts centre; the products were the result of painstaking work by children and staff throughout the term, as part of their curriculum studies.

Enquiry task I

List the art forms that feature in the brief description above.

Try to identify where they feature in the National Curriculum for Key Stages 1 and 2.

Make a note of any aspects of the arts which you think are not included.

The nature of the arts

We identified the following four issues as crucial in examining our attitudes to, and professional practice in, the arts:

- how we define the arts; what is particular and special about them, and why arts teaching is important in the primary school;
- how *consuming*, studying, experiencing and appreciating artists' and artistes' work, informs children's own creative endeavours, and how *making*, or practical experience, helps them access and understand the work of artist practitioners;
- whether a 'combined arts' approach enhances or limits children's potential within each arts form or discipline;
- how analysis of features common to the 'artistic process' within the various art forms can inform planning and implementation of a broad and balanced arts curriculum in the primary school.

To provide a context within which to examine these issues, we will track the contribution of one class of primary children to the school's arts event, introduced above, through the rest of this chapter.

Defining the arts

In different ways, appropriate to their communities and the curriculum, most schools undertake 'arts focused' work. The very title of this book assumes that there are subjects which can be called 'the arts', although what can and cannot be included is debatable. There are many preconceptions about what is, or is not 'art'; the definition tends to become blurred at the edges. You may or may not think of yourself as an 'artist', 'craftsperson' or 'designer' when choosing colours to decorate a room. You may or may not see disco dancing or synchronised swimming as 'creative'.

Whether or not there is a common understanding of what is regarded as art, rather depends on those involved in any discourse around the subject. Perhaps the debate is most fierce among those who participate in the arts themselves. A useful definition is offered by Suzanne Langer, who defined 'art' as:

❛ *[. . .] the generic term subsuming painting, sculpture, architecture, music, dance, literature, drama and film . . . the practice of creating perceptible forms expressive of human feeling.* (Langer, 1958, p. 87)

The Arts in School Project Team (1994, p. 138) defined those processes by which humans make sense of experience 'by representing it in symbolic form' through the arts as *visual, aural, kinaesthetic* and *enactive*; although not each term applies to all the arts. You can probably think of several arts activities you have worked on with children which covered some or all of these processes. Consider Langer's statement that 'some works of art are given to the imagination rather than to outward senses'.

> *A novel is usually read silently with the eye, but is not made for vision, as a painting is; and though sound plays a vital part in poetry, words even in poetry are not essentially sonorous structures like music. Dance requires to be seen, but its appeal is to deeper centers of sensation. The difference between dance and mobile sculpture makes this immediately apparent. But all works of art are purely perceptible forms that seem to embody some sort of feeling.*
>
> (Langer, 1958, p. 87)

Despite these differences, it is indisputable that the term 'the arts' stands for a particular aspect of the way human beings behave, respond and make sense of experience, and that feelings are involved. Inevitably, difficulties of definition arise, for example, whether 'photography' is a branch of the 'visual arts' or subsumed within 'media studies', and whether dance can be separate from music. Some forms of creative endeavour defy categorisation: a film of a Japanese operatic performance with puppets clearly combines many forms. Later, we examine more fully how an analysis of differences and common attributes within art forms can help the teacher in the primary classroom.

It is possible to be affected by an experience without fully understanding it. Without linguistic competence, we cannot read, understand or appreciate literature and poetry, whereas visual and musical art forms are perhaps more universally accessible. It may not be possible fully to grasp the significance of Australian Aboriginal dance and music, without some knowledge of the cultural values and histories it depicts and represents. Such a performance can, nonetheless, appeal directly to our senses, can promote enjoyment or a less positive response.

> *Aboriginal art may be functional, serving practical, spiritual or ceremonial purposes, but, like other art, it also reflects the personal and distinctive manner of the artist. It reflects the values of the culture in which the artist lives, and it is often understood only by a limited and informed audience.*
>
> (Kowanko, 1994, p. 13)

There is a debate about whether or not an understanding of one art form can inform the appreciation of another. While being a good flautist does not make you a good pianist, let alone a good water-colourist, it is argued that an appreciation of the process through which the creative artist works has a common factor in all the arts forms mentioned above. For teachers, the relationship between knowledge about, and appreciation of, arts subjects is a matter worthy of serious consideration.

> *There are two general ways of engaging in the arts. Individuals can be involved in producing their own original work, and in responding to existing work. We refer to these two respectively as **making** and **appraising.** Both are of equal and fundamental importance in arts education: each is important in itself and each can stimulate and enrich work in the other.*
>
> (Arts in School Project Team, 1994, p. 140)

The arts take many forms, which have common links, bonds or qualities. For ease of reference, we have adopted the following list of 'arts disciplines':
- creative writing (literature, poetry);
- visual arts;
- drama;
- music;
- movement and dance;
- 'new media' (photography, film, television, computer art).

The arts in the primary school curriculum

The National Curriculum makes clear distinctions between the arts. Music and art are considered separately, drama and 'media studies' are subsumed within English, and movement and dance happen within PE. We would argue that the arts are, in common with all core and foundation subjects within the National Curriculum, to do with learning, consolidating and applying skills and knowledge, describing and recording experience, and the continual process of coming to terms with and understanding the world. The arts truly apply across the curriculum, to *describe, create, express* and *inform* aesthetic responses.

To consider how active engagement and practical creative work complement each other within the primary curriculum, we return to the school's arts week.

Case Study 2

A second-year undergraduate student worked with a class of five-year-olds in the school, under the guidance of the class teacher. Both of them were very keen on the potential offered for developing work towards the arts week, and eager to begin the process of planning and preparation. The student needed to find out about the children's understanding of 'creative arts', and which aspects of the animals topic she would need to teach. She consulted the teacher, and found out what the children knew about dance, drama, art and music, as well as about animals, through structured interviews, and by consulting records for their previous two terms in school.

Meanwhile, she collected a range of resources: reference texts, wildlife magazines, videos, reproductions and photographs of artists' work and stories about animals. The classroom became a resource base, so children could research, investigate and build on what they already knew. An 'art gallery' was created of artists' paintings and photographs of animals. Goldfish and giant snails on loan from the local college were the centrepieces of the science area, and the 'menagerie' (previously the 'home corner') was equipped with stuffed toys, puppets, ornaments and books, a tape recorder with headphones, and tapes of animal noises and music.

Enquiry task 2

Think how you might set about researching the current levels of understanding of pupils you teach, perhaps through a structured interview. How might you find out if any of them has any special aptitude or training, such as attending dance classes? How will you find out about their knowledge and understanding of concepts associated with living creatures?

Present a series of animal pictures, and animal noises, to children. Ask them to identify similarities and differences. Note any characteristics they comment on, and then group the responses to inform you of what understanding they already have. Did any responses surprise you? Did any children have particular knowledge, or particular difficulty?

Like life itself, the arts happen in two and three dimensions, but also in time, which has been described as the 'fourth dimension'. Time is needed both for the maker to make and for the viewer or listener to experience. What might be termed 'static' visual art, such as drawings, paintings and sculptures, enable viewers to visit and revisit, for example a gallery or school hall, and decide for themselves how long to stay. Stories or poems take time to read or to listen to, but can be tackled piecemeal. Film, television, music, theatre and dance performances require the full attention of the audience for the duration of the event. Teachers may use excerpts from books or performances, or reproductions of works of art, but if this visual equivalent of the soundbite is all children ever experience, the importance of scale and setting is lost. Without some experience of the whole, children are unlikely to grasp the significance of the excerpt. Time is, therefore, a vital dimension in arts teaching.

The student in the case study above considered this in her planning. She aimed to provide not only tools and materials for practical work, but inspiration and information about the subject matter, animals, for them to see, hear and experience at first hand and through use of a range of media, to learn about appreciating, as well as doing and making, within the arts. This means having a view to the longitudinal nature of planning, as well as breadth and depth. The various stages through which the children would have to work were charted to help keep track of events, and to ensure everything would come together at the right time. As you read on, you may be able to identify these stages, which will be discussed more fully towards the end of the chapter.

'Making' and 'consuming' the arts

Most adults and children associate with the arts, either as 'makers' and/or as 'consumers'. Most able-bodied children watch and listen to music and performance as part of everyday life. Given the opportunity, most children willingly use tools and materials to draw, paint, model, make sand pies or indulge in pretend play, experiment with sounds and try out different body movements. We are all aware of how children of all ages imitate pop stars and cartoon characters in their play. Indeed, the large numbers of adults who indulge in singing to kareoke machines might indicate that this behaviour can by no means be called 'childish'.

Whether or not this is 'making art', 'theatre', or 'dance' is not at issue here. But it is from these generally agreed 'natural' actions that creativity develops, and can be nurtured and taught. As well as practical skills, learning to see, learning to listen and how to be a member of an audience, teachers have a responsibility to help children become discerning, active consumers, able to engage with the arts at all levels in an informed and critical way.

Despite protestations, heard by the authors with astonishing regularity, of both students and teachers, that they 'can't do art', or 'know nothing about the arts', it is likely that every reader has recent, relevant experience within the arts.

Enquiry task 3

Make a grid like the one below. Note on it if you personally have recently actively engaged in an arts activity, either as a 'maker' or as a 'consumer', for example:

Artform	Making (being an artist/artiste)	Consuming (being in the audience)
Creative writing		
poetry	writing	reading
literature	writing	reading/listening
Visual arts		
arts/crafts/design	making an artefact	visiting a gallery/museum
drama	playing a role	watching a play
music	singing, playing	listening to music
movement/dance	dancing	watching dance
New media		
photography/	using a camera	looking at photographs
film/TV/video	using a video camera	watching TV/video/film

List the criteria you used to decide whether something was or was not 'art'. Decide where you can apply the descriptions *visual, aural, kinaesthetic, verbal* or *enactive*.

You may have surprised yourself with just how much, and how often, you engage with the arts as a creative pursuit, or as a member of an audience. There might well be obvious links, in that your choice of participation in arts events mirrors what you yourself like to do within the 'creative arts', that is, if you are a member of an amateur or professional drama organisation, you may find that watching theatre is a major leisure pursuit.

Probably all artists and artistes have gained some of their inspiration from the work of others in a similar field. While direct copying is rarely appropriate in primary schools, the acknowledgement of how excellence inspires and motivates greater understanding, effort and achievement, is as important here as in the professional arts sphere. Linking the experience of seeing and hearing accomplished professionals' work to children's own practical creative work is perhaps not so easy as the National Curriculum for Art implies:

 They investigate visual ideas in making images and artefacts, making connections with their own work. (QCA, 1998, p. 14)

The need to engage with the arts both through self-expression, and as an observer or listener, is recognised in the National Curriculum orders for art and music, which place statutory obligations on schools to provide opportunities for children to experience the work of artists and musicians. Although modified in the publication, *Maintaining Breadth and Balance at Key Stages 1 and 2*, (QCA, 1998) quoted above, these requirements still stand: linking 'Listening and Appraising' with 'Performing and Composing' in music, and 'Knowledge and Understanding' with 'Investigation and Making' in art.

No such links are mentioned in PE. Although performance, including dance, is given 'the greatest emphasis' (QCA, 1998, p. 18), there is no requirement to introduce children to the work of skilled practitioners. We tend to agree with this statement.

> *In order to develop dance appreciation it is also important that children also see good quality dance performances by professional companies or others of an equal standard, preferably in a theatre where the atmosphere can enhance the imaginative experience.*
>
> (Roberts, 1988, p. 55)

In English, at Key Stage 2, 'pupils should be given opportunities to participate in a wide range of drama activities, including improvisation, role play, and the writing and performance of scripted drama' (NCC, 1995, p. 11), but there is no requirement for them to experience performed theatre. Many teachers nevertheless try to provide experience of professional theatre and dance, using video, inviting local dancers to school or arranging visits to performances.

Think back to the case study, and consider whether children would be inspired or daunted by jointly viewing and discussing live or videoed performances, or making visits to galleries and museums, and trips to the farm or zoo. Of course, not all such experiences can, or need to, be directly linked with current work in class, but can stand alone, as valuable, thought provoking, intense and satisfying or challenging events.

The potential and limitations of 'cross-curricular' approach

Where teachers can capitalise on combining aspects of the arts, and other areas defined in the National Curriculum, streamlined planning can be supported by cross-curricular work. Below, we revisit the student from the case study above, to see whether a 'combined arts' approach can enhance the whole, rather than diminish each of its components.

Case Study 3

With the 'arts' focus in mind, the student listed relevant art forms, and thought about what resources, or 'input' would help the children with their work, or 'output'. Curriculum areas overlapped; observing and drawing animals would inform creative writing and dance, but would not teach how to write a poem or make music. She took her ideas to her class teacher, who helped her to prioritise, to make planning more manageable. Her notes read as follows:

Creative writing

input
- to read and listen to animal poems and stories, including tape recordings;
- to photocopy favourite extracts, poems and pictures to make a class anthology;
- to use the CD-ROM information package to look up information about the animals;

output
- to write stories, poems and factual pieces;
- to use word-processing packages to draft, revise and publish the work.

Visual art

input
- to study photographs, to observe how familiar animals look from different angles;
- to record in sketchbooks observations of fish and snails etc.;
- to look at videos and slides of animals on a hand viewer;
- to browse storybooks, animal magazines, art books and reproductions of artists' work;
- to compare different pictures of similar animals;

output
- to draw and paint the animals from firsthand observation and from video;
- to use the drawings as a basis for printmaking;
- to make clay models of animals;
- to make their own puppets with animal characters;
- to use a graphics package on the computer to draw and colour animal images.

Music, movement and dance

input
- to observe the animal movements and forms in still photographs;
- to watch videos of ballet, carnival, Indian, African and Aboriginal dance about animals;
- to listen to music depicting or representing animals;
- to listen to recordings of animal sounds, on tape and in video;

output
- to mimic the shapes and movements of animals from the visual reference;
- to develop dance sequences from these movements;
- to make music for their dances using voices, instruments and computers.

Drama

input ■ to watch excerpts of cartoons and other videos depicting animal characters;

■ to watch a performance of a local theatre-in-education group;

output ■ to improvise conversations between the goldfish;

■ to use the 'home corner' props, especially the puppets, in imaginary play;

■ to link dramatic exploration and improvisation with movement and dance.

Photography, film and television

input ■ to watch videos of animals in wildlife programmes and in cartoons;

■ to sort and write commentaries on family photographs;

output ■ to take photographs and make videos of the animals;

■ to take photographs of themselves in animal poses and guises;

■ to make videos of advertisements for pet foods.

Enquiry task 4

Missing from the list, as you may have realised, are teaching and learning aims. Using National Curriculum documents, identify teaching aims appropriate to the class you are working with at the moment. You might find the planning chart below helpful.

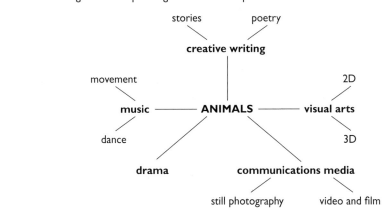

There is often a temptation to provide lots of ideas, and to encourage children to try out a bit of this and a bit of that. There may be a place for this type of work on occasion, but it should not be at the expense of planning for depth as well as for breadth. The student needed to pace her planning over a term, to ensure continuity and progression in each of the distinct art forms, as well as gaining knowledge and understanding about animals. We all know from personal experience that it is hard to learn something properly without time and practice, without opportunity to develop ideas and skills, and the chance to make a few mistakes on the way.

Planning for process

This is important in all areas of learning, but particularly so in the arts, where we now try to offer a way of planning to cater for the necessary 'process' to ensure both sound learning and satisfactory 'products'. To help define this process, we go back to the classroom, for an account of how the work progressed, based on the teaching aims you have probably identified.

Case Study 4

The next stage of the work was creative and to some extent unpredictable. There was an explosion of activity, which had to be recorded and assessed. Children's verbal observations of what they had seen and discovered were recorded by the teacher or assistant in notebooks. Drawings were kept in sketchbooks. Favourite illustrations were photocopied, and, with pictures from magazines and cards, pasted into a series of scrapbooks, labelled according to categories determined by the children, such as wild or pet animals, very big and very small animals, farm animals. Thus the children made their own reference books, and the 'pig' page alone illustrated just how many types of pig existed, apart from Miss Piggy or the standard cartoon image. Sorting, classifying and recording information would be useful for future reference during the project.

The children took sketchbooks (not worksheets) to the zoo, to make notes of their observations, some of which focused on patterning of animals' markings, some on shapes of legs or manes, some on lines, the curve of trunks, tusks, feet and beaks. Back in school, the teacher photocopied sample drawings and grouped them, to illustrate how many ways there are of responding to such an exciting stimulus as being in the presence of real animals. They also took tape recorders to help them remember the noises, although BBC tapes were more useful back in the classroom.

'Imagination' and 'creativity' are often assumed to be part of childhood. In practice, for children to imagine can be quite difficult. Adults have a lifetime's experience, direct and vicarious through film, television, literature and so on, on which to draw. If the arts are 'a response to our thirst for knowledge, insight and revelation', requiring 'abilities to question, explore, collaborate and extend and develop one's ideas' (OFSTED, 1998, p. 4), children need suitably interesting and challenging stimulus and experience as starting points.

Reflection 1

Think of how each activity listed above informed the different arts activities outlined earlier. Which, for instance would be useful in helping the children write stories, make paintings, and create dances?

From the start of the animal project, the student initiated a process of research, and helped children to record and organise their findings. They were not expected to know everything before they started, but encouraged to develop their knowledge and concepts through learning about how to access information and ideas from the resource materials offered. Such research is sometimes a conscious part of the creative process, for example when writers set out to learn all they can about the setting, potential characters and likely plots for a new novel.

The work of art does not begin when pencil touches paper or fingers strike keys; the life experience of the composer or artist, the time spent learning skills and knowledge, the ability sensitively to respond to experience and events, all contribute to the work of art in its final form. The artist's work can be a painful process, which requires application, and often many reworkings and revisions of the original idea. When work itself comes quickly to fruition, it is usually because it is a distillation of long periods of gestation. It is said that Handel wrote the *Messiah* in twenty-eight days. This would be just about enough time physically to write the notes on paper, without taking account of the creative process, amendments and reworkings. But Handel was not working from scratch: ideas, themes, melodies and potential arrangements were already in his mind.

The National Curriculum for English at Key Stage 2 suggests a series of 'stages' through which a piece of writing passes from start to finish.

> *To develop their writing, pupils should be taught to:*
> - *plan – note and develop initial ideas;*
> - *draft – develop ideas from the plan into structured written text;*
> - *revise – alter and improve the draft;*
> - *proofread – check the draft for spelling and punctuation errors, omissions or repetitions;*
> - *present – prepare a neat, correct and clear final copy.*   (DfE 1995, p. 15)

The National Writing Project (1990) describes 'a writing process':

starting → composing → revising → editing → publishing → evaluating

The Arts in School Project Team (1994, p. 143) offers the following steps in an artistic process:

exploring → forming → performing → presenting → responding → evaluating

The implication in each of these examples is that children need to learn *how to go about* doing something as well as *how to* do it. Skills acquired, of organisation, researching, designing and developing ideas can be applied in future to other projects. However, for most of us, to 'plan' is not quite that simple. To 'start' can be the most difficult part of the process, as anyone trying to tackle a difficult assignment, or to write a sensitive letter, appreciates. Of many analyses offered to help teachers plan classroom work, we find the following most helpful in relation to arts planning. It was devised by Peter Woods to describe a 'process' model for classroom work. We have summarised it; the reader is recommended to read the original text.

- **Conceptualisation:** *beginning the process; inspired thought;*
- **Preparation and planning:** *clarification of aims, assembling resources;*
- **Divergence:** *explosion, an innovative/creative stage, unpredictable;*
- **Convergence:** *integrating, products of previous stages examined;*
- **Consolidation:** *refining, writing up, editing, performance, etc.;*
- **Celebration:** *end; exhibition, performance, book, concert, film showing, etc., acknowledging achievement, air of excitement; end of event, a 'rite of passage' out of 'criticality' and back to 'normality'.* (Woods, 1994, p. 173)

As you read about the progress of the children in the case study, you may already have identified some of these 'stages'. Such a longitudinal approach to planning helps teacher and children to keep tabs on how a major undertaking is progressing. Nearly all classroom work constitutes part of a major undertaking. If children are to learn about, as well as experiencing, the 'creative process', teachers need to give due attention to the different stages through which they travel as they respond creatively to learning and experience. Time can then be allocated, so that each stage is given its own value, as well as contributing to 'end products'.

The stages may involve *active* or *reflective* processes, with *technical* or *organisational* assistance and guidance from the teacher. Some may be a combination, for instance, editing is *technical* but is the outcome of a *reflective* process. They are not necessarily linear; more often they are, and perhaps should be, cyclical.

The first stage, 'conceptualisation', the beginning of the process, and the second, 'planning', clarifying aims and assembling resources, have already been considered. We left the student in the middle of the third, 'divergence', the innovative, sometimes unpredictable stage. This is perhaps the most exciting, the most challenging and the hardest to handle. To the outside observer, it can seem rather anarchic, because it is at this stage that ideas are being formulated and tested, arguments tend to happen, and feelings run high.

'Never show a fool or a child anything half-done' is an old Chinese proverb quoted at one of us when younger children expressed horror about the messy heap that was 'A' level work-in-progress. Disorder is almost always a stage in any form of work. Most of us are familiar with the moment of despair when ideas are too few or too many, notes seem irrelevant and we see no way of making any sense of the chaos, which Nias (1989) refers to as a 'seed-bed for creativity'. Experience teaches that this is the time to stop, temporarily, and try to organise. The process of tidying, making room to carry on with the next stage of operations, can itself give a sense of satisfaction, and become the spur to the next stage. The teacher needs to recognise the signals, and to ensure that these moments are used productively, as an opportunity to assess how much has been done so far, to help children to organise valuable exploratory work in sketchbooks, notebooks and scrapbooks, and to identify useful strategies for taking the work forward.

Planning the product

It is at this later stage that 'convergence' takes over, where children and teacher together make sense of progress to date, reorganise, revise and clarify what has been achieved and begin to see where editing and modification will be necessary in order to achieve a satisfactory product. Ideas may have to be discarded, perhaps shelved rather than forgotten. Editing is an important aspect of composing, in any creative medium, and learning how to do this is a difficult but necessary task.

Case Study 5

For the children working on the animals theme, the process of composition, based on personal and group experiences, in turn motivated further research. They had focused on aspects of growth, and from this had emerged some ideas for a presentation of poems they had written, together with movement sequences, based on hungry animals, not just caterpillars, but snails, rabbits, goldfish, elephants and sharks as well.

If children could not quite get the movement they aspired to in PE, they could look again at a video or photograph, or the real thing, if they had one, before the next session. Movement sessions themselves informed descriptive writing; words like 'writhing' and 'lumbering', used by their teacher, appeared in their own writing.

They **learned about** drawing, movement, poetry and music as well as **doing or making** it, through the overarching theme of animal movement. Each piece of work informed the next and they could, arguably, be done in any order. There were parallels with how 'real' cartoonists, painters, sculptors, actors, musicians and dancers work; children were able to make connections between the work of artists and their own.

Modification of ideas is informed not only by a personal critical look at achievement to date, and inviting the views of others, but also by additional inspiration and stimulus offered by the teacher. Most people need to review ongoing work, whether it is a letter to a neighbour or a poem. (The letter to a neighbour might be a poem, but there's another matter.) To recognise the need to revisit and work through an idea is vital in planning. This is often cited as the most difficult aspect of teaching to manage, and some of us have spent too much of our professional time chasing up 'unfinished' work. It can be very liberating to recognise that this may indicate that too many tasks have been set, with too little time allowed, rather than that children are not working fast enough.

When children are in a quandary, or 'stuck' or even in despair, they might take a break and use it to look again at a particular book, or painting, or listen to a piece of music, to help them carry on. In drama and PE, children 'warm up', 'rest' and 'cool down' at different times. It may be equally important to recognise this rhythm of work in other aspects of our planning, in more academic areas of work such as creative writing or making art.

Case Study 6

The children then revised and developed their work in art, music, dance and creative writing. There was some pre-recorded and original music to represent each kind of animal, the movements of each had been almost perfected, the book of poems neared completion, and the artwork was hanging up to dry.

Final revision and rewriting can be a tedious process, but the introduction of additional stimulus was something the teacher had foreseen as necessary at this stage. Children looked again at artists' work and videos of dancers portraying animals they had now seen. They were delighted to notice new things in what they looked at, and to hear new sounds and effects in what they listened to. The educative process of the last few weeks had sharpened their perceptions, and increased their understanding of the significance of certain symbolic representations they had previously experienced, but understood less. The revision process enabled them to use their knowledge and understanding to respond to personal experience, and to appreciate how artists work from both personal feelings and research.

In the 'consolidation' stage, gradually, but in the control of the teacher, the ideas and thoughts get pulled together, and fine-tuned for the deadline. Rehearsals, often thought of as only relevant to the performance arts, are equally necessary in presenting exhibitions or displays of work. The arrangement, layout and setting have to be tried out and considered, to make sure the message is getting through to the intended audience. Costumes for performance need to be looked at from a distance, the props and scenery need to be clear. Music must be heard. The same sort of criteria apply to visual presentations.

This stage needs particularly adept timing, so that the children can perfect their work to an optimum level, but not be so bored with it that they flag. This is less likely if the process has been streamlined, so children work collaboratively towards a series of worthwhile, inter-related 'products', rather than being pressurised into mass production without the benefit of consolidation, modification and fine-tuning.

Then, all too soon, the deadline nears, and its very proximity leads, more often than not, to a new injection of energy and activity, as the celebration of the term's work comes towards its fruition, described at the beginning of this chapter. The class we have tracked were to read their carefully crafted poems to a musical accompaniment, against a backdrop of paintings and drawings they had made of the animals depicted in words, music and visual art.

Case Study 7

The children made their way excitedly to the hall, clutching their poems and paintings, giggling with anticipation as they saw children from other classes in animal costumes and carrying weird and wonderful puppets. The performance for the parents was a great success. The children talked about it for weeks, and watched the video the teacher made, so they could see themselves from the front. The teacher evaluated the work in her file under subject headings, and levelled the work according to the descriptors in the National Curriculum such as 'speaking and listening', 'writing', 'reading' and 'life processes and living things'. The children just remembered how wonderful it all was.

Defining the issues

This chapter has probably raised as many questions as it has addressed, but in conclusion, it may be helpful to summarise the four key points established towards the beginning.

First, there are identifiable areas of experience, contained within the National Curriculum 'subjects', that can accurately and usefully be defined as 'the arts'. These have much in common, notably that they encompass the practice of creating and appreciating forms expressive of human feeling. They represent different ways in which humans respond to and make sense of the world in general and personal experiences in particular.

Second, children need opportunity to engage with both 'creating' and 'consuming' the arts. For children to learn in, through and about the arts, they need stimulus and first-hand experience to respond to, and to be taught ways of articulating their responses, both for themselves and for others. Children also gain motivation and inspiration from experiencing the work of professional artists, designers, musicians, actors, film-makers and photographers, and others in the creative arts field. To provide experience of the arts, as a focus for developing critical and creative faculties, is to a large extent the responsibility of the school.

Third, some aspects of the arts can usefully be labelled 'cross-curricular', although each art form or discipline makes its own demands. Children need to be taught each as a discrete area of the curriculum, as well as appreciating both 'overlap' and 'combinations', fully to participate as makers and critics at their own level. Study skills may not seem an appropriate focus for the youngest of our schoolchildren. However, working within a cross-curricular, combined arts approach develops children's understanding of how to manage and organise their own endeavours, leading towards more independent decision-making and 'ownership' of ideas and products. Without this, it is debatable whether creativity of any kind can happen, especially in the classroom. The research process, which led to arts products, also embraced furthering of understanding of life and life processes, environmental influences on animal and human existence, change and growth, and promoted an appreciation of the mystery and meaning of life.

Fourth, making performances and exhibitions demands time and space, makes noise, and generally challenges classroom organisation, especially during those parts of the process where everything is unformed and untidy. There is in all areas of the curriculum, but perhaps particularly in the arts, a definable process through which the product emerges. Each stage needs further input, additional research and inspiration, or sustained work on major projects can be rather tedious. Stages described by Woods (1994) as *conceptualisation; preparation and planning; divergence; convergence; consolidation* and *celebration*, can prove helpful for facilitating the process of planning and implementing work in the arts in primary classrooms. The final celebration is of major importance. Both teachers and learners are likely to find their hard work more rewarding when it is shared, enjoyed and perhaps admired.

References

ARTS IN SCHOOL PROJECT TEAM (1994) 'Teaching the arts', in BOURNE, J. (ed.) *Thinking Through Primary Practice*, London: Routledge, pp. 138–47.

DEPARTMENT FOR EDUCATION (DfE) (1995) *Key Stages 1 and 2 of the National Curriculum*, London, HMSO.

KOWANKO, R. (ed.) (1994) *Aboriginal Art and the Dreaming*, Adelaide, Australia: Department for Education and Children's Services.

LANGER, S. (1958) 'The cultural importance of the arts', in ANDREWS, M. F. (ed.), *Aesthetic Form and Education*, Syracuse, NY: Syracuse University Press, pp. 1–18.

NATIONAL CURRICULUM COUNCIL (NCC) (1995) *Key Stages 1 and 2 of the National Curriculum*, London: HMSO.

NATIONAL WRITING PROJECT (NWP) (1990) Walton-on-Thames: Nelson.

NIAS, J. (1989) *Primary Teachers Talking*, London: Routledge.

OFFICE FOR STANDARDS IN EDUCATION (OFSTED) (1998) *The Arts Inspected: Good Teaching in Art, Dance, Drama, Music*, Oxford: Heinemann.

QUALIFICATIONS AND CURRICULUM AUTHORITY (QCA) (1998) *Maintaining Breadth and Balance at Key Stages 1 and 2*, London: QCA.

ROBERTS, T. (ed.) (1988) *Encouraging Expression: The Arts in the Primary School*, London: Cassell.

WOODS, P. (1994) 'Chances of a lifetime: exceptional educational events', in BOURNE, J. (ed.), *Thinking Through Primary Practice*, London: Routledge.

Further reading

MOYLES, J. (ed.) (1995) *Beginning Teaching: Beginning Learning in Primary Education*, Buckingham: Open University Press.
This collection of writings, illustrated by examples of classroom practice, investigates what it is to be a competent and effective classroom teacher. It considers the complexities of modern primary teaching, with a most helpful chapter on the arts by Maurice Wenham.

HOLT, D. (ed.) (1997) *Primary Arts Education: Contemporary Issues*, London: Falmer.
The writers concern themselves with both everyday practice and broader issues which relate to arts education in the primary school, in particular the creative aspects of the English curriculum, and identifying some of the challenges which confront the primary arts teacher today.

ISHERWOOD, S. and STANLEY, N. (1994) *Creating Vision: Photography and the National Curriculum*, London: Arts Council of Great Britain.
'This book provides a sound conceptual framework and useful working tool for all those interested in working with photography and electronic media across a range of classroom subjects' (Lord Palumbo, in his foreword). It also contains a host of useful references and addresses for teachers to contact for information and resources.

Part II   Art forms

Chapter 2

Drama: narrative as a unifying theme in the arts
Mary Kear

Introduction

This chapter considers the role of narrative in both current educational practice and the arts, and discusses some ways in which narrative themes can unify arts provision and provide valuable learning experiences for children in school. It begins by suggesting that narrative forms permeate much of what children experience generally, before turning to the particular role that narrative plays in the arts, and in teaching and learning. This is explored further through two case studies that describe classroom situations and children's work. Finally, the chapter offers a rationale for the contribution that arts events with narrative themes make to children's learning.

Teachers use narrative processes widely in their practice across the primary curriculum, because they are familiar forms of social communication that children understand and respond to. Narrative, the telling of stories with words, still or moving pictures, movements and sounds, forms the basis of much human communication. Giving an account, relating a series of experiences, chronicling the events that led up to a situation and reporting the consequences, are part of the everyday conversations that children hear, as is the receipt and assimilation of and response to the narratives of others. Narrative is inherent in informal and official communications between people in both private and public situations. It is an essential part of the way families and friends share cultural knowledge, and build social and personal relationships. Children participate in or are aware of this dialogue in whatever form it takes.

Narrative is an essential element of many of the cultural frameworks that children experience. Historical events are recounted to them as stories and this seems to help them place themselves in time and make sense of their past. Information about personal and cultural histories ('Tell me about when you were a little girl, Mummy') consolidates children's understandings of who they are and contributes towards the construction of their individual identities. As is well documented, the effects of losing one's personal identity or having part of it denied, can be profound.

Traditional stories continue to survive in children's literature, and even though many describe situations far removed from current experience, the telling and retelling of these narratives to succeeding generations endures, creating a sense of continuity and a link with the past. A visit to the children's section of a bookshop or library will confirm the continuing popularity of many of these.

> *Often stories have been approached through different art-forms, and indeed, re-worked or adapted for new generations. An example of a well-known story in the European tradition would be Cinderella. . . . The 'bones' of the story have been adapted time and time again in the theatre and in books and form part of the range of stories of which most European children are aware. . . . Non-European cultures boast an equally rich fund of stories that have been retold and written over many years. . . . The Cinderella story itself, though simple, raises all sorts of questions about personal morality and family life, and the fact that it has been reworked so often suggests that there is something of long-term interest in the tale.* (Tambling, 1990, p. 1)

Enquiry task I

Write a list of the stories you remember liking as a child. Visit a school library, classroom book corner or the children's section of a bookshop and see how many of these are still available and popular. Ask some children about their current favourites and compare lists.

Today we have access to scientific knowledge about a range of natural phenomena and scientific and technical processes, but stories persist as a way of offering children explanations about aspects of their lives that cannot be rationally explained.

The popularity of science fiction with children demonstrates the power of narrative to build pictures of what could and might be in the future. Sacred texts and holy books preserve narratives that provide the basis for the beliefs, tenets and rituals associated with some of the world religions that children may experience. Narrative strategies are extensively used in media and entertainment for children and adults. Many interactive CD-ROMs provide children with a narrative or choice of narratives. Television programmes and books on a range of topics use personalities, settings and stories to transform humdrum activities into the exotic and extravagant. The news bulletins that children may see are personalised and contextualised to increase their impact and validity. Narrative reports that they include give information about the lives and aspirations of those who live elsewhere in the world and the 'storying' of these increases their poignance and our ability to empathise.

Stories, fables, chronicles, legends and romances feature in all the arts that children are familiar with: literature, film, theatre, dance and the visual arts.

> ❛ *Throughout time, the arts have represented one of humankind's most potent means of giving expression to, and communicating ideas and concepts about profound issues to do with the human condition – issues of birth, life and death made manifest through sensory exploration of the world we inhabit. Individuals are able to understand themselves more fully by coming to terms with their identity and uniqueness through arts experiences. Profound ideas concerning the spiritual, political and social are made manifest through the arts in ways which cannot be expressed and made apparent by other means.*
>
> (Taylor and Andrews, 1993, p. 1)

Since narrative is evident in so many areas of our life,

> ❛ *[. . .] we dream in narrative, daydream in narrative, remember, anticipate, hope, despair, believe, doubt, plan, revise, criticize, construct, gossip, learn, hate, and love by narrative.* (Holt, 1997, p. 60)

and people always seem to organise and arrange their environments in a way that is aesthetically pleasing for them, we might ask if there is a relationship between constructing and understanding narrative and the way in which we think; does this link with the use of the story in primary school?

Narrative processes are commonly used in school because they are associated with tried and tested teaching and learning strategies. Teachers read, tell and retell stories about the past, present and future. They may dramatise, personalise, sequence, chronicle, illustrate and contextualise subject content to support learning, because they know that children respond positively to these strategies and they have found that working in this way helps children to think and learn.

For a child, the intellectual demands of participating in an exchange of narrative, where they receive and decode verbal information, depend on the use of a range of cognitive skills and processes. Construing meaning from written narrative also requires the employment of a diversity of skills from the young reader in finding congruent meaning and constructing an inner reality that accords with that of the writer. Constructing a spoken narrative also makes demands on junior authors and in turn contributes to their understanding and cognition. Retelling an episode can act to refine the experience, a distillation through which a clearer understanding of what happened, and the sequence of events as they occurred, is achieved.

> *Narrative, conceived as a primary act of mind, has long been held to play a central role in making experiences meaningful.* (Holt, 1997, p. 55)

Telling or writing stories, where invented situations and characters are developed into narratives that attract and communicate meaning to the reader, requires linguistic and literary skill and expertise.

It seems then that the use of narrative plays a significant role not only in the social and cultural life of children, but in the way they create, communicate and think.

> *Thus if the story is seen to be part of our everyday events and actions it should also be viewed as an explicit resource for intellectual activity.* (Holt, 1997, p. 39)

Narrative also characterises much of children's imaginary and social activity. They use narrative in their collaborative and solitary play, much of this located in what can be described as arts activities. Children construct and dramatise social situations with their peers, engaging in role-play, pretend and make-believe. They create settings for and stories about their toys. Their paintings, drawings and modelling usually have a narrative content and the process of making them is often accompanied by a spoken or sung, imagined narrative.

Although for many children television, video and computer-based activities, are now the major source of narrative content, story-telling and story-reading still remain an important part of the relationships they have with other children and adults at home and at school.

The role of narrative in education

Narrative is the basis of many of the activities that teachers plan for their pupils to carry out in school. They are encouraged to tell, write and illustrate stories, and use narrative processes to record accounts of investigations, describe special experiences and report particular processes. These are central to the educational process (Holt, 1997, p. 33).

In the arts in primary schools, children enact stories through music, dance and drama. They portray their experiences graphically and make painted, drawn, printed, sewn, constructed and modelled images to represent situations. Narrative processes are central to all these activities.

Enquiry task 2

List the forms of story-telling that occur across all areas of the curriculum in one week in a classroom you know. Indicate which of these include visual art, drama, dance, or music.

Then, consider the narrative and arts content in the case study below that describes a programme of work that took place over a school term in a mixed Year 5/6 class.

Children's learning through narrative and the arts

Case Study 1

The Underground

'The Underground', a class topic for the Spring Term, was planned with the intention of promoting awareness of 'what lies under our feet – animal life, technological systems, natural resources, and how we respond to and use them'. Included in the work covering this topic were the following selected examples with a narrative emphasis, many of which were, in addition, arts activities:

- investigating myths and legends associated with 'The Underground' as represented through the arts, for example, The Labyrinth and the Minotaur; Peer Gynt; Aladdin; Ali Baba; The Witch of Wookey Hole; Orpheus in the Underworld;
- close examination of certain texts that described underground settings, such as *The Hobbit*; *The Wind in the Willows*; *The Animals of Farthing Wood* (revisiting a previous class serial); *Fantastic Mr Fox*; *Memories of a Speedwoll Miner* (current class serial);
- creating text (poetry and prose) on an identified theme associated with 'The Underground' and for an identified audience;

- using the story of the spiral; finding out about Fibonacci and his number system;
- identifying rock specimens and charting their life histories;
- constructing a geological chronicle of the area of the school;
- visiting 'Big Pit' (a mining museum) and hearing the story of the pit from guides who had been working miners themselves;
- preparing and engaging in a debate over the past history, current situation and future predictions for the mining industry;
- listening to, analysing and subsequently composing folk songs with a mining theme;
- considering the relationship between miners' work and mining communities and comparing with children's own experiences;
- listening to music on the theme of 'The Underground';
- composing music on the theme of 'The Underground';
- preparing and performing a dance drama to present an aspect of the life of a miner;
- making monoprints of miners;
- making models of miners from clay.

In the case study above, narrative forms were used across the curriculum, to support the processes of communication and cognition essential to teaching and learning. In English, a range of texts associated with the class topic was presented to the children. The teacher intended to develop their understanding of different genres in literature and of the relationship between these stories and the culture and time in which they were written. The stories were read or told to the class and others were placed on special display in the book corner for individual reading. Comparisons of some of these texts provided the children with information about how individual authors used language to create a sense of place, atmosphere and action. They looked for evidence of the intentions of writers in relation to audience and story content. Activities analysing narrative structure and storyline were intended to lead to greater appreciation of the complexity and diversity of story-telling.

Memories of a Speedwell Miner (Moss, 1986), read as a class serial, was the first experience of autobiographical writing for most of the class. The teacher's original intention was to read only extracts, pre-reading having indicated that some parts might be too dull. But the children's interest in this account of real and recent experience meant that most of the text was read. The book also made for useful comparison with the previous class serial, a fictional story, with opportunities to discuss the depiction of reality in texts ('Is it true, Miss?'), and the communication of moral messages through fiction.

All these activities acted as resources and preparation for the children to create their own texts. They wrote poetry or prose on themes they identified, but associated with 'The Underground'. Readership was identified from the beginning, so that style, content and presentation could be structured accordingly. Writing was initially in draft form, with an option later to proceed to a finished piece which could be a reading to be performed with musical accompaniment (voice or instrument) or an illustrated, word-processed text. There were also opportunities for collaboration, for example, co-authors working together on a text, illustrators and musical accompanists working with authors.

A large collection of rocks, fossils and minerals soon built up in the classroom, some from those already in school and from the teacher's own collection and others brought in by the children. This assortment generated much interest, becoming one of the major resources of the topic. Children never seemed to tire of presenting a new 'find', giving an account of its discovery and, after close examination, discussion and argument, placing it alongside similar examples. Initially groups of children carried out sorting activities with the collection.

These were structured to challenge ideas and motivate discussion, and proved to be an essential stage in building topic knowledge. Later, with reference to books, the samples were identified and classified, 'life histories' were charted, and information was stored on a computer database. Careful and detailed observation was carried out with magnifying glasses, and observational drawings made to record the results of this scrutiny. These drawings were then developed into designs for print blocks, and used to print cover papers for topic books.

The collection contained a number of fossil ammonites of different sizes, textures and colours. The children were fascinated by their spiral shape and also by information they had found in a reference book. This explained that the shape of the ammonite was mathematically identical to the spiral shape of shells, cones, the centre of sunflowers and other natural structures. They were then introduced to the story of Leonardo Fibonacci, the Italian mathematician (1170–1250) who developed a number system known as the 'Fibonacci sequence' that, when represented as mathematical points within an area, created the same shape as the spiral in the ammonite.

A walk around the local area provided some geological and geographical evidence that was used, along with reference books and charts, to develop a geological and geographical chronicle of the school area and find out how the features of the localities influence the nature and locations of human activities within them (DfEE, 1995a).

A class trip to 'Big Pit', a former coal mine functioning as a museum and visitors centre, was scheduled to take place in the middle of the term. The trip was arranged at a time when the children had already been involved in the project for several weeks, and so had amassed an amount of knowledge and information that could usefully inform the experience of going down a coal mine. At Big Pit, the children were guided by ex-miners who gave practical, geological and historical information and told stories about their own experiences when working there as miners.

With some weeks left after the trip, advantage could be taken of the excitement generated by this dramatic experience. On returning from their visit, the children made pictures of miners in monoprint. They were familiar with this print technique, enjoying the immediacy and fluency associated with using it. In addition they made models of miners from clay, again a medium in which they had developed both skill and expertise. These art activities drew directly on the impact of the visit to the mine. The experience of going down in the cage into the mine, equipped with helmet, light and battery, was clearly reflected in the quality of the prints and models. The effect of the autobiographical stories related to them by their miner guides was also evident in the narrative that the children brought to their own artwork, through their definition of character, action and setting.

In addition to the experience of preparing for and visiting a real coal mine and reading about the experiences of a local miner related by himself, the children were told stories by the teacher about her own family, stories she had been told as a child. Her grandfather had been the engine-winding man at a Somerset pit, responsible for operating the 'cage', the lift that transported the miners at the beginning and end of each shift they worked, and for their safety during this hazardous descent and ascent. Listening to these stories led to discussion about the conditions in which miners worked, the communities in which they lived and current news stories concerning mining. A series of debates was set up to present and argue issues. The use of narrative had acted throughout to make information accessible and relevant to the children.

Children listened together to music with themes associated with 'The Underground'. *Peer Gynt* (Grieg), *Orpheus and Eurydice* (Offenbach), the

Fossil Dance from *Carnival of the Animals* and *Danse macabre* (Saint-Saëns), were analysed and compared to identify the way in which composers used sounds and structures to achieve an intended effect, such as to create a particular atmosphere, (DfEE, 1995b). Cassettes of the music were placed in the book corner alongside a listening centre for individual listening.

Composing music on the theme of 'The Underground' followed, children choosing to work either collaboratively or individually, performing finished pieces to the class. Folk songs, with lyrics that documented and commented on social events, were unfamiliar to the children. A folk-singer, parent to children in the school, was invited to talk to the class about, and perform, folk songs associated with mining. The children listened to these and other versions on tape, and subsequently tried composing their own folk songs with a mining theme.

A dance drama on an aspect of, or incident in, the life of a miner and his family, was prepared over several weeks. This grew from the children's interest in the class serial, *Memories of a Speedwell Miner*, and their burgeoning knowledge about the dangers and historical associations of the mining industry. Previous dance/drama had been carried out using a tape-recorded radio programme, where contrasting social situations had been used to inspire movement and dialogue. The teacher's intention was to encourage a more independent and less prescribed approach, while focusing the children's attention on some of the situations and relationships portrayed in the text, so developing greater understanding and empathy. Narrative gave both the inspiration for, and structure of the work.

The arts and narrative forms pervaded all these study areas, although many were also inter-disciplinary. All had elements of narrative form which proved effective in engaging the children's interest and maintaining their motivation. Dance, drama, the visual arts and music all contributed in different ways to the growth of knowledge, expertise and understanding that gradually developed as experiences, interacted with and informed each other. For example, scrutiny of samples of rock with magnifying glasses and then further examination during observational drawing, built up knowledge of surface texture, pattern, form, shape and mass. This developed familiarity with the samples that helped when the children were determining ways to measure these in mathematics. A unifying process of integration was in place to support learning.

Reflection 1

The teacher's role in narrative arts events

Note that children were
auditioned for parts in this play.
- What selection criteria would
  you think appropriate and fair
  in this situation?
- What might have informed
  the teacher's choices?
- What dilemmas may have
  arisen as a result?

Case Study 2

Fantastic Mister Fox

'Fantastic Mr Fox' was a school play performed to an invited audience at the end of a school year. A professionally written script, based on the book of the same name by Roald Dahl, was used, and children from all classes auditioned for parts, and if selected for a role, learned the part by heart. The performance was in the school hall, where scenery was erected at one end, and an area of the floor served as the stage. Costumes and props were made by parents, and animal masks were designed and made by children.

The scenery consisted of a painted backdrop representing 'underground', with the top section as a shadow screen. This was used to represent 'above ground', with shadow shapes attached to the back of the screen to imply setting, and changes of lighting indicating time of day. In addition, part of the play where mechanical diggers dug away the hillside under which Mr Fox and his family were hiding, was dramatised with shadow puppets and sound-effects.

During the play, action behind the shadow screen was the responsibility of one class of Year 5/6 children and their teacher, and involved many of the opportunities for learning through narrative and the arts as described above.

The teacher's role was crucial in the planning, resourcing and management of this project, and in encouraging positive and productive participation by all the children in the class. All aspects of the process were the result of careful consideration and planning, for example: the introduction; the way the sessions were structured and tasks set; demonstrations of techniques; the pattern of the period of work itself; interventions by the teacher during work; the finishing and clearing up arrangements; evaluating and reflecting on what had happened during each session ready to proceed to the next; and finally the performance itself.

The class was influenced by the enthusiasm the teacher herself felt for the project. She saw the potential of a situation where classroom activity involving everyone could be developed according to a brief (the requirements of the story and dialogue), and in response to the ideas of the children, and presented legitimately as a product for public consumption. As Tambling puts it, 'A real task has a purpose, a deadline and a natural outcome' (1990, p. 16).

During the initial introduction of the project to the class, a clear outline was given of various parts and supporting activities, and the production and performance itself, so that the children were able to recognise the potential of the situation. The script of the play was read and discussed in relation to the original book. The narrative, a familiar text regarded highly by the children, framed the task and gave structure and continuity.

Planning allowed for sufficient time at the beginning to revisit shadow puppetry. Real examples of shadow puppets and reference books were consulted to demonstrate possibilities, revise scientific and technological principles and show the relationship between the stories and their realisation on screen. Techniques were demonstrated and the children experimented, trying out ideas and approaches. Cutting an accurate and fluent line, drawing with scissors, needed practice to create the crisp outlines necessary for effective shadow shapes.

The script for *Fantastic Mr Fox* was reread to establish framework, criteria and the demands of the narrative. General discussion produced initial ideas. Then a selection process identified those most suitable and workable, and groups were established to take responsibility for designing scenery, puppets, and creating sound-effects. Regular reference back to the story and/or the script checked the appropriateness and relevance of the work as it developed.

Enquiry task 2

In a school, identify all the spaces traditionally used for arts activities. Add to these other areas that could be rearranged or combined to be made suitable.

Finding appropriate space in which to work, always a difficulty in arts activities in primary schools, led to a search for available and suitable areas. In the case study above the classroom was rearranged to accommodate the necessary practical work for a number of different and contrasting activities. A shadow screen with a mirror in front was improvised to try out designs, practise manipulation of the puppets and explore lighting effects.

The actual performance date, arranged some time ahead, made the teacher's time management particularly important. The children needed enough time at the beginning of the process for research and experimentation. After this they needed time to generate, select and refine ideas and then to realise them practically. It was also essential to leave sufficient time towards the end for rehearsal and practice.

[. . .] logically, only the individual child can be the agent of his or her own learning. This means that in the daily practice of good teaching the child must be given space to select, to judge, to innovate, to initiate, to ask questions, to explore. (Taylor and Andrews, 1993, p. xii)

But this process did not always fit comfortably into the available blocks of time. The dilemma was to work within the time-scale, while not allowing it to restrict or inhibit activity, but recognising what was possible in terms of processes, materials and time.

Collaboration, practical activity, active learning, inventing and imagining, all characteristics of this arts activity, required a distinctive working environment. Much collaborative work was involved and this meant an exchange of ideas, debate and discussion. This, along with the level of practical activity involved, meant action, movement and noise. So an additional concern of the teacher was to establish a mode of working and a classroom ethos that generated an acceptable level of noise and control, while effectively supporting the activities.

Preparing for *Fantastic Mr Fox* gave opportunities for cross-curricular work that combined, developed and consolidated the children's knowledge of techniques and processes associated with technology, science and art, and covered National Curriculum requirements in these subject areas.

There were also benefits in other areas of the curriculum, particularly English and mathematics. Making judgements about quantities, working with space and form, transferring three-dimensional forms to two-dimensional shapes, applying their measuring skills in a range of purposeful contexts, all involved the children in forms of mathematical thinking. Expressing ideas, negotiating solutions to problems, managing the social and practical aspects of performance, all contributed to oral fluency. The intense concentration required to take part in the performance certainly improved listening skills, and the dramatic interpretation of a familiar story developed greater understanding of the structure of that text.

Evaluation, carried out by both children and teacher in the classroom, during the preparation and making stages, was supplemented by further assessment later on, when access to the hall and working in the 'proper' environment behind the big screen, was possible. At this time new problems emerged, for example, about the best position for lighting and where best to stand to manipulate the puppets to ensure that no shadow from puppeteers could be seen.

The rehearsal and performance themselves introduced a new set of experiences. Incidents at rehearsal showed that good pre-performance preparation was essential, to check everything was ready and in place, and that everything worked. The children also had to be quiet for long periods and aware of the sequence of events happening in front on stage, so that cues could be responded to promptly, and references in dialogue reflected on the shadow screen immediately by them. Collaborative skills were stretched to their limits in restricted space accommodating children, puppets and equipment, and needing to allow for movement and manipulation.

Good self-control and co-operation were the only ways to ensure success. There was evidence of significant personal development in some children as they responded to the demands and challenges of the experience, learning to control their own reactions and responses, to channel their excitement and frustration and share the general sense of pleasure and achievement at the end.

Children's learning through arts events with a narrative theme

What were the real advantages of working in this way for the teacher, and what did the children learn through being involved in projects that unified arts activities and used narrative themes? Arts activities offer learning experiences for children through combining subject areas and associating knowledge and skills. These activities facilitate delivery of the National Curriculum rather than restricting it, as demonstrated in both case studies described above.

 So making art supports intellectual, social and emotional development, while offering children opportunities to develop essential subject-based skills, knowledge and understanding that can also apply across the rest of the curriculum.

(Callaway and Kear, 1999, p. 2)

Enquiry task 3

Select two subjects in the National Curriculum. Study the content of one of the case studies described in this chapter and identify areas of the National Curriculum that are covered in the relevant Key Stage.

 In the HMI series Curriculum Matters: The Curriculum from 5 to 16 *(1985) certain broad headings for skills learning are introduced. These include*

'communication skills', 'problem-solving skills', 'creative and imaginative skills', all of which are well served by an integrated pattern of learning that cuts across subject boundaries. . . . The same publication also suggests that 'Skills are best acquired in the course of activities that are seen as worthwhile in themselves. Arts projects always are and bring with them a context for learning.

(Tambling, 1990, pp. 2,3)

As Tambling makes clear, opportunities for learning abound in any project where the arts are combined and motivation is high. It is certainly the case that children usually approach arts activities eagerly and enthusiastically, seeing them 'as worthwhile in themselves' and valuing both the processes and products. Narrative content in no sense detracts from this response, in fact the presence of a storyline usually acts to stimulate children's interest further and increase their enthusiasm for becoming involved.

The relationship between effective learning and motivation is acknowledged and it is our experience that when children are excited, involved and enthusiastically absorbed in their work, as they were at times in both case studies, they learn more productively.

 Yet when all the arts come together on these occasions, learning can be discernibly enriched and enhanced. Increased levels of motivation and involvement bring a renewed sense of purpose into the classroom.

(Taylor and Andrews, 1993, p. 181)

Through arts projects, teachers can exploit this enthusiasm to encourage participation in a range of valuable learning situations. In the examples described above, children were using different tools, equipment, environments and processes, to express themselves, their ideas and observations and doing this with developing confidence. They made choices about the suitability of resources for particular tasks, at times being decisive and at others hesitant, selecting or discarding material and ideas, experiencing both leadership and direction, and taking responsibility, all learning experiences that may have acted to enhance their self-esteem. Engaging in the range of individual and collaborative work involved, helped the children develop a critical, evaluative attitude towards their own arts work and to the ideas, processes and products of other artists, and contributed to a sense of achievement. In these situations children were working with first-hand, practical, sensory experiences.

 The arts are closely related to the senses and these are at their most acute and impressionable during childhood.

(Taylor and Andrews, 1993, p. xi)

The activities required them to generate, develop, process and represent ideas, while evolving collaborative and personal modes of expression. They identified, responded to and found solutions to problems, and developed and refined the practical skills associated with the use and control of materials and equipment. 'Skills need to be taught, but in an embedded context, which relates to what children strive to do' (Bruce, 1987, p. 57).

Both case studies offered differentiated experiences that enabled children to participate at their own particular level of competence. These activities often took the form of open-ended tasks where outcomes were not specifically defined. Even where products had to meet specific criteria, as in the shadow puppets, enough flexibility existed to accommodate different levels and qualities of contribution.

This chapter then, suggests that classroom practice where narrative becomes a unifying theme in the arts, should be applauded, and the significant contribution it makes to children's learning, be acknowledged and celebrated.

 Stories, then, act as mediators of language and culture to children entering a new world – the classroom.   (Gregory, in Holt, 1997, p. 33)

References

BRUCE, T. (1987) *Early Childhood Education*, London: Hodder and Stoughton.

CALLAWAY, G. and KEAR, M. (1999) *Teaching Art and Design in the Primary School*, London: Fulton.

DfEE (1995a) *Key Stage 1 and 2 of the National Curriculum: Geography*, London: HMSO.

DfEE (1995b) *Key Stage 1 and 2 of the National Curriculum: Music*, London: HMSO.

GREGORY, R. (ed.) (1987) *The Oxford Companion to the Mind*, Oxford: Oxford University Press.

HOLT, D. (ed.) (1997) *Primary Arts Education*, London: Falmer Press.

MOSS, F. (1986) *Memories of a Speedwell Miner*, Bristol: Bristol Broadsides.

TAMBLING, P. (1990) *Performing Arts in the Primary School*, London: Blackwell.

TAYLOR, R. and ANDREWS, G. (1993) *The Arts in the Primary School*, London: Falmer Press.

Further reading

HOLT, D. (ed.) (1997) *Primary Arts Education*, London: Falmer Press.
In this 'review of the current situation with regard to primary arts provision', different contributors offer personal responses to issues associated with the arts in primary schools in the years since the introduction of the National Curriculum. These range from theoretical discussion to description of classroom practice, presented in a form that is accessible and informative.

TAMBLING, P. (1990) *Performing Arts in the Primary School*, London: Blackwell.
A comprehensive guide to the title. The contribution that the performing arts make to children's learning, and the benefits of including them in the primary curriculum, are strongly argued. The idea that these activities should be the province of specialists is challenged and practical suggestions and advice about every aspect of planning and provision for the performing arts, bring them within the capabilities of every classroom teacher.

TAYLOR, P. and ANDREWS, G. (1993) *The Arts in the Primary School*, London: Falmer Press.
The last volume in the excellent series *The Falmer Press on Aesthetic Education*, this book includes chapters on both the theory and practice of the arts in primary schools. In the process of offering a rationale for the arts and describing examples of good practice, the text covers a range of issues that concern teachers in delivering the arts in primary schools.

Chapter 3

Music education: elements for personal, social and emotional development
Jane Tarr

> ❝ *I know my function within a society which embraces us all is to continue an age old tradition . . . to create images from the depths of the imagination and to give them form whether visual, intellectual or musical. For it is through images that the inner world communicates at all.*　(Tippett, 1974, pp. 155–56)

Music is about sounds and silences. Examples of musical composition and performance can be found within every cultural grouping of the world. It seems that the creation and performance of music is a basic human process. Although it exists everywhere, different communities place different emphases on particular aspects of sounds and silences. Music is a means of communication and as such it is a symbolic language. The actual meaning conveyed is often quite abstract and subject to personal interpretation but sounds begin to take on meaning according to how they are experienced within different cultural contexts. The sound of a large group of violins has often been used to incite the feeling of romance for people rooted in a European tradition. The rhythmic pattern which opens the end of the theme tune to television's soap opera *EastEnders*, catches our attention, even if we are out of the room, and seems to anticipate a dramatic event. Our perceptions of films are greatly influenced by sounds and silences, for instance the motif/phrase used every time the shark is required in the film *Jaws* by association incites fear and suspense, even with no view of the huge beast itself!

This chapter aims to support the development of readers' musical understanding through exploration of our personal and emotional responses to music: through acknowledgement of the social and cultural contexts in which music is heard, and through introducing the reader to the basic elements of music. By considering appropriate starting points for a spoken/written language through which to discuss music, we can consider how, as teachers, we can develop musical understanding for pupils in the elementary stage of compulsory education.

Music and emotional response

We all listen to music for a variety of different reasons. Some pieces of music are special, for instance pieces we use to calm ourselves or which excite us into action. Music surrounds us. Television and the radio bring music into everyday life providing a multiplicity of sounds from different styles and genres, carefully chosen for specific purposes. Advertising uses music to attract attention and to link a musical phrase with a brand image, thus creating an identity which, by association, leads to higher sales of the product. Music is used to imply romance, to create a sense of suspense or evoke specific atmospheres. There are instinctive musical sounds and phrases which incite a similar response from human beings rooted in very different cultural backgrounds, for example: slow and low sounds are of a darker mood whilst fast and high sounds might be happier. Common responses to sounds do occur but people are broad and varied in their responses to the variety of different musical genres found in a wide variety of different contexts. Music is often present at social occasions, religious ceremonies or sports events and has the effect of encouraging or promoting cohesion between people. It is a powerful form of communication.

A recent radio item described an innovative idea to reduce the threat of violence from young people gathering in the local train station and to encourage travellers. The music of Delius was played through a sound system, because research had indicated that today's youth did not like listening to it. Hearing Delius at the station would discourage gatherings of this age group whose mere presence was deemed threatening to older travellers. The results of this experiment are not known.

In the Barcelona Metro, Baroque music is played to passengers as they wait for trains or walk through the station and the connecting pathways, which, it is believed, both calms impatient passengers waiting for their trains and eases the disquiet associated with walking through a long, enclosed corridor.

These examples of music used to evoke contrasting feelings and emotional responses are interesting in that they respectively exploit positive and negative attitudes to music. The first example reveals how young people often 'wear' the music that they like and wish to be associated with, as a badge. To be seen listening to Delius would not fit in with their youth culture and so they might move away from the train station. Whilst Baroque music carries less obvious cultural association, it is in itself calming and comfortable for most people within the Western European tradition. It is important that we as teachers, understand why and how these feelings are evoked in us. They will be personal and subject to our own experiences of sound and will reflect our life experiences of music and sound. As teachers we need to consider the experiences of music that children bring to the classroom. It is from this starting point that a music education begins.

The notion of an emotional response to music raises an important issue, often debated within arts education, concerning the arbitrary division between the affective/feeling and the cognitive/reason domains of human experience. The philosopher, David Best, writes fervently about this division, which he regards as a myth exploited by arts educators, which serves to devalue the position of the arts in education. He argues that since there can be no cognitive learning without emotional response, division between the two is quite meaningless because:

 [. . .] the kinds of feelings which are the province of the arts are given only by understanding, cognition and rationality. They are not possible for a creature incapable of such cognition. (Best, 1992, p. 7)

Our emotional responses to music and sounds are important to record and map conceptually. A particular piece of music might make you cry. Why? Is it because of the time you first heard it? The quality of the sounds heard? The ups and downs of the melody? The speed of the piece? The piece of music has incited a response and this could be caused by a number of reasons. Some are concerned with the nature of the sounds themselves, others are concerned with the social and cultural experiences surrounding the hearing of a piece of music, which lead to a series of associated meanings becoming attached to it. Music is a highly complex symbolic language and the meanings that children and adults attach to it can be drawn out through playing, engagement in composition and appreciation of sounds heard.

You may find that using words to describe an aural experience is difficult. Children will also find this difficult as they develop the language to describe

Reflection 1

Listen to a favourite piece of music. Write down as much as you can about:
- why it is important to you;
- what you like about it;
- the kinds of feelings and responses which are aroused in you as you listen;
- the sort of context in which you feel the music might be best experienced.

their own responses. It is difficult because you are involved in the process of transferring from one mode of representation (music) to another (words), which is called transmediation. Your initial response will probably be an emotional one. In order to communicate this clearly to another person you need to be able to talk about the music using spoken language. Speech describing music cannot equate to the heard experience, but serves to allow humans to explain the effect in some way to another. If the other person has also heard the piece of music then the sharing and comparing of talk about the piece can become more meaningful. Swanwick has explored the notion of musical knowledge which he says is a form of analysis but combines with an intuitive response to sounds heard (Swanwick, 1994). In order to communicate one's understanding or knowledge of music, a spoken language will be required. The later sections on the elements of music attempt to provide the reader with a basic vocabulary for talking about music.

Musical sounds of the *mbira*, a Zimbabwean metal-tongued instrument played with the thumbs and index finger of both hands, incite a response from the listener which occurs without any understanding of the social or cultural setting in which the music was originally composed. The capacity for music to incite such responses illustrates that music has 'a degree of symbolic autonomy' (Swanwick, p. 170) and the meanings attached, being usually culturally transmitted, are as clear as other symbolic languages. This would be similar to hearing a poem in a strange language yet nevertheless finding meaning in the sounds, pattern and expression of the words. One's response to music will be personal and intuitive, an emotional response which can be articulated. Children can be encouraged to talk about their feelings for music in a range of genres and explore what they like and why it is that they like it. Alongside this perception is the social and cultural context: the layer of meanings that become attached to music forms a part of children's social and cultural development alongside learning about the specific techniques and skills involved in performing or composing music.

Social and cultural context of music

Music can be heard in a range of contexts – the home, the concert hall, outdoor festival, the pub, many workplaces, the supermarket, the underground, celebrations, funerals, religious events, entertainment events and to support important cultural occasions. A community often will use music as a medium to set the 'tone' at social events such as parties, discos, pubs, shopping centres and swimming pools. In relation to the school community the experience of music will again occur in a variety of settings:

ranging from individual, small groups, whole class, whole school events, involvement within the local community, to county events and reaching into more global musical understandings. Consideration and experience of the various contexts for music is an important element within the music curriculum.

Music education has the potential to provide a route into greater understanding of difference and similarities between cultures (Oehrle, 1996). Bob Marley sang throughout the struggle for liberation in the Caribbean, against the oppression of others. The emotions expressed were powerful and many people from a range of different cultural backgrounds found and still find solace in his music. One of the most unifying global musical events of the late twentieth century was in 1985 when Band Aid charity concerts linked five continents via satellite for a day; millions of people heard the same music programme. A similar event recently linked choirs world-wide singing Handel's *Messiah*.

The social aspect of music adds a further learning dimension, enabling communication and collaboration to take place, often across spoken linguistic barriers. Through the expansion of information and communications technologies, people of the world can communicate more directly, facilitating the sharing and reproduction of a wide variety of musical styles and genres. Thus music can be a link between people from many different backgrounds, providing a rich and unique mode of communication. David Elliott writes that 'if music education functions as culture . . . then it may also have the potential to change prejudicial attitudes and behaviours' (Elliott, 1989, p. 14). This is a lofty claim but suffice to say that the listening to and appreciation of a range of different styles and genres of music, has the potential to enhance one's understanding of others.

Enquiry task 1

Listen to your favourite piece of music again. Find out what you can about:
■ the social and cultural setting of the music;
■ the actual sounds heard and how they are made;
■ the performer;
■ the style of music.

Consider how you might incorporate this knowledge into your teaching.

When exploring the wealth of music available, you may find it useful to refer to the *Rough Guide to World Music* (Broughton *et al.*, 1994) a text which provides a brief yet comprehensive outline of the range of known musics in the world and information about the cultural and social settings in which they have developed.

Musical understanding requires some research into the context from which sounds have emerged, combined with an understanding of the expressive quality and the basic elements and structure of the sounds. It is through the development of musical understanding that one is able to 'lift music out of being a simple sensory pleasure and into the realm of discourse' (Swanwick, 1994, p. 39). Once we are able to engage in this discourse, the challenge of music education becomes less daunting. We should always remember our own pleasure and joy in listening to and performing music. An analysis of the Beatles song *Yesterday*, serves to illustrate a developed level of musical understanding expressed in words.

> The lyrics conform to the principle of nostalgia fundamental to the sentimental ballad as a musical genre, the use of the string quartet backing can be understood to signal that this song 'aspires to the condition of art', the use of the acoustic guitar can be understood to impart a serious 'folky' feel and the more formal melodic, harmonic, rhythmic and timbre features of the sounds as music can be interpreted in ways that are not yet clear to underscore the feeling of loss occasioned by the song.   (Shepherd and Wicke, 1997, p. 10)

The combination of a number of different cultural reference points may in part account for the phenomenal success of the Beatles; elements of various sorts of popular music were harmonised and the new music appealed to a wide range of tastes. Encouraging children to talk about music in this way is not always the aim of music education. A fluency in the use of sounds and instruments in performance and in composition is sought. These skills are the practice of the musical language which can only be found in music-making. However a basic vocabulary can be beneficial in the classroom to enable children and adults to discuss their musical experiences.

A basic musical vocabulary

To engage in discourse about music, to increase awareness of what it is about, how it is created and why one has different responses to it, a basic vocabulary is required. As with any vocabulary it can only be learned through practical application of the concepts, through creating sound compositions and discussing them as well as listening to a range of different music and talking about it. Further research about the concepts increases our and children's ability to discriminate aurally. Learning and using language generated by this process can lead to a more pro-active involvement in musical experiences. Understanding the elements of sound is one route to providing the building blocks of a musical language which will enable practitioners to talk about concepts experienced through performance, composition and listening to music. This chapter now addresses each of the musical elements in turn, with a brief explanation and suggested practical activity to enhance your understanding. It must be acknowledged that the elements listed are interdependent and one cannot be isolated from another. However for our purposes it is useful to focus on one at a time.

Timbre

Throughout time humans have demonstrated a desire to create sounds and have explored their environment and its materials for their sound-making potential. The nature of the sounds created or quality of the sound, known as timbre, is affected by what there is to work with: the materials to make instruments or the voice. The steel drum, created from beating out discarded oil drums, provides a very different range of sound potentials from the bamboo whistle which is made from the stem of a plant with carefully carved holes: each has a different timbre. The difference between your vocal sound and anyone else's is also concerned with timbre, the quality of sound.

The enormous range of instruments that humans have devised to create sounds can be categorised as follows.

- *Aerophones* are instruments in which the sound is produced by the vibration of air and include whistles, mouth organs and piano accordions.
- *Idiophones* are instruments made from naturally sonorous material formed in a variety of shapes, made to sound in a variety of ways. This category includes instruments that are hit (xylophones), shaken (rattles), scraped (washboard), plucked (*mbiras*), rubbed together, hit together, or stamped on a hard surface.
- *Membranophones* are instruments in which the sound is made by the vibration of a stretched membrane or skin, examples being the many forms of drum that exist today.
- *Chordophones* are instruments in which the sound is made by the vibration of strings in any form – bows, harps, violins, guitars and pianos fall into this category.
- *Mechanical and electrical instruments* include instruments which make their sound through the use of electricity or mechanical processes. Examples of this category include the musical box, electric guitars and electronic keyboards.

These categories outline the variety of sources of timbre or sound qualities that exist in our world. Children respond well to listening carefully to sounds within their environment. The use of a tape recorder on outings or trips can enhance aural discrimination.

Case Study 1

A class of Year 5 children on visiting their city centre took a tape recorder. A pair of children collected all the sounds they heard from taxi doors slamming to ladies' heels clicking. On return to school they wrote a whole class poem entitled 'Sounds of the city'. This written text then formed the stimulus for small group compositions. A further session involved a group writing a song using the poem which also incorporated sections from other group compositions. A City Symphony emerged over the ensuing weeks, which was performed at the end of the term involving the whole class in singing and playing instruments.

This activity illustrates the detailed exploration of timbre and took children into both performing and composing from an initial starting point of environmental sounds.

Enquiry task 2

Explore your environment for materials which can produce sound. Attempt to create or collect an instrument of each type described above. Assemble a group of friends and ask each to experiment with one or several of the instruments. Tape the sounds you make and ask other friends to guess what materials created each sound. Make a note of the responses and then play the tape to a group of children. What differences do you notice in the responses?

Pitch

Singing is the best introduction to understanding of pitch. Vocalisation involves physically moving up and down in pitch. High and low sounds offer contrast in terms of pitch. In Medieval Western Europe, notation was developed by monks who wrote down the pieces performed by choirs in churches. They first focused on the melodic line which was sung. In the early eleventh century, horizontal lines were introduced to provide more accurate indications of *how* high and *how* low. Notes took on different shapes to indicate how long they lasted. The importance attached to pitch and tuning in Western music can be traced back to the beginnings of this notation (Britten and Holst, 1968).

Rhythm

Listening to natural living forms provides an ideal introduction to rhythm. The repetitive wave motion of the sea and the human heartbeat are both examples of movement and sounds which occur regularly in time. The consistent pulse or beat can be organised in different combinations such as groups of two, three, four, five, six, seven etc., with a pause or a strong beat to emphasise the beginning of each group of beats. Much Western popular music is based on the repetition of four regular beats, but other musics have different rhythmic groupings. Some African music contains quite complex rhythmic patterns which are layers of simple rhythms gathered together or superimposed. When a Ghanaian drummer visited a school, he gave each small group of pupils an apparently simple rhythm to play repeatedly. As each group joined in, in turn, there developed an impressive complexity in the rhythmic whole.

Dancing is a spontaneous and vital physical response to music. Young children in particular make actions to music, which is an important way of learning to experience rhythm. From very small babies jiggling about to music, to the role of dance in a community, the relationship of movement to a style of music is evident. The smoothly flowing arm and body movements of Asian dancers reflect the fluid music. In contrast, stamping and marching and stick-brandishing echoes Morris Dancers' very rhythmic music. Studying dance music alongside the traditional movements associated with it promotes an understanding of how rhythm can be physically experienced.

Texture

Texture is about how different sounds and patterns can be layered onto each other. The term 'texture' describes the density of the sounds assembled: the number of musical lines played together is the essence of texture. A string quartet with just four players has a different texture from that of a whole orchestra with over forty players. Texture may vary within a piece of music. Sometimes, many lines of music come together; at other times they will enter one by one, or just a few may be played together. A rock band might start a piece with the bass guitar playing solo, after which the drums enter, followed by the guitar, then the voice enters with the words for the song and finally everyone is playing together. This demonstrates the texture of music, and how the different parts are layered together. When you teach a simple song such as *Frère Jacques* or *London's Burning*, divide a group of singers into four groups each group with a different line from the song. Perform the piece, starting each group at the beginning of the appropriate line. This is called a round and illustrates layers of sound performed together.

Dynamics

The changes in the volume of music, the loudness and the quietness of its sound is known as dynamics. Encouraging pupils to perform both quietly and loudly for different occasions can help them to understand dynamics. Getting gradually louder or gradually quieter is more complex and can usefully be related to an environmental phenomenon such as the train leaving the station. Often a singing group knows when it is musically relevant to grow louder. The volume of sound made by a group of people alters in relation to the need to express something. A good example is the way the singing of fans grows louder at a football match when the ball reaches the opposing team's goal. Alternatively, you might assemble a group of pupils and attempt to produce the sound of a rainstorm. Try passing a quiet clap around the circle making it progressively louder with each revolution, then gradually quieter again, thus demonstrating the gradations in dynamic quality.

Tempo

The speed of sounds, or tempo, also varies in different contexts, the speed reflecting the nature of the meaning that is being expressed. A romantic sentimental ballad will frequently be a slow set of sounds, compared with a dance piece for a celebratory festival with a more dynamic, faster tempo. Appreciating the time and pace of sounds is a crucial aspect of musical understanding. Saint-Saëns' *Carnival of the Animals* (1886) has several movements representing different animals, whose varying speeds of movement can be heard in different parts of the piece.

Enquiry task 5

Listen to 'The Elephant' and 'The Aviary' from Saint-Saëns' *Carnival of the Animals* and make notes about the contrasting tempo and instrumentation. Provide a group of children with simple percussion instruments. Ask them to create two contrasting pieces of music, one which is fast and one which is slow in tempo. Discuss the differences with the children.

Structure

Most pieces of music are structured in time. At its simplest this means that a piece of music, like some types of writing, has a beginning, a middle and an end or an introduction, a development and a conclusion. Recognition of repetition is a preliminary step to a fuller understanding of musical structures. Many songs and pieces use repetition of melodic lines or rhythmic patterns. It is useful to devise ways of recording the structure of a musical piece so it can be more easily understood as a whole. The simple form of a 'question' followed by an 'answer' is frequently used in music and is particularly evident in some African musical traditions. The round, where separate parts play the same melody but start in rotation, like *Frère Jacques*, introduces another simple form in music. Many different musical styles use the *ostinato*, a musical pattern that repeats over and over again whilst other patterns are played simultaneously. Usually the ostinato can be heard in the lower part as the basic structure to the music.

Enquiry task 6

Listen to a short piece of music:
- Mozart Minuet in G, or;
- a Cornish folk song, or;
- a familiar nursery rhyme, or;
- an excerpt from Ravel's *Bolero*.

Attempt to record:
- elements of repetition within the melodic line, or;
- the rhythmic patterns used.

Label sections A, B, C, etc., for ease of explaining the repetition used.

Through following the tasks and carefully listening to some of the suggested music, the music teacher and learner can gain a deeper understanding of each of the musical elements described above. The language which can be developed through exploration of the elements will enhance the ability of music teacher and learner to listen to music with understanding and also to be able to create pieces of music of ever-increasing quality and complexity.

Teaching and learning music

We each have our own musical preferences, and, through listening to a variety of different musical genres and styles, can move closer to understanding exactly why a certain kind of music is particularly appreciated. Attempting to express and explain why we like a piece of music helps us to develop our appreciation and understanding further. The musical elements provide a framework for talking about music, and also for appreciating, creating and describing musical structures. There is a body of knowledge, skills and concepts in music that can be explored and learned through practical participation in the performance and composition of music.

The affective aspect of music and the specific techniques and skills cannot easily be separated, so teachers need to understand their own musical preferences in order to help children to understand theirs. A useful framework for arts pedagogy was developed during a course organised for artistes and teachers working together in school (Tarr, 1996). Through an analysis of the working process of musicians and artists, six areas emerged which also serve to provide a framework for arts teaching. These cover the following:

- a context/environment conducive to work;
- time for free exploration with materials/ideas/concepts;
- stimulation from external sources;
- specific skills and techniques;
- time for reflection;
- presentation of the work.

A context/environment conducive to work

The appropriate context depends on the aspect of music being addressed, but it must always be an environment where children are prepared, and able, to listen. This can present logistical problems in school. The corridor, the hall or an empty room may be spaces where small groups can make sound which does not distract others from working. Facilitating careful listening, away from distractions, can be even more problematic. The requirements depend on the nature of the teaching objective.

There are occasions when individual learning is best, as when children are practising instrumental skills. Group work may be the best context for exploring a selection of sound-makers, devising a group piece or rehearsing an instrumental accompaniment for performance. The whole class can often work together when a song or a musical game is used to teach a musical element. Technology can help, for instance the use of an electronic keyboard with headphones and a recording facility.

Children benefit from listening and performing in different locations, such as in church for the carol concert, or a theatre as an inspiring venue for a musical production. Also relevant here are the social aspects of music, such as sharing a concert with local residents. Inter-school liaison is both valuable and feasible through shared musical events, such as secondary schools visiting or inviting primary feeder schools to share musical performances. Performing or hearing music in local halls or other buildings can bring greater understanding of the role of music in the community.

Music education uses a variety of different and contrasting approaches to teaching and learning. A didactic instructional approach is relevant for some aspects and an exploratory, learner-focused approach is most relevant for others. An appreciation of the potential range of teaching approaches is important for teachers, who have to decide which approach best suits them personally, along with the best approach for achieving the specific learning objective stated.

Time for free exploration with materials/ideas/concepts

Tarr's research showed that teachers are more inclined to shorten the aspect of arts pedagogy that focuses on the open-ended, unstructured element of a session. The role of 'play' in arts education:

> [. . .] *represents to the child the externalised expression of his emotional life and therefore in this aspect serves for the child the function taken by art in adult life.* (Lowenfeld, in Abbs, 1987, p. 40)

To be able to express feeling through sound, children need to explore a range of sounds, and their potential to evoke particular responses. This experience and experimentation leads to fuller understanding of the raw materials of music-making. A further advantage in providing time for free exploration is that children can learn at their own pace, rather than being over-directed. Given clear instructions and appropriate resources, small groups can work independently, away from the classroom. Such free exploration with sound often enables children to consolidate their knowledge of the processes of composition or performance. The tape recorder is useful to record results, such as the three best sounds produced when exploring a particular instrument, or a simple chant put together around a theme.

Stimulation from external sources

Basic essentials for good musical education include a broad and varied selection of instruments which produce sound in many different ways, which children can investigate and thereby learn how different materials make sounds. Instruments traditionally used in different parts of the world, as well as recordings of them in various contexts, provide additional stimulus. Resources gradually accumulated soon grow into a wide-ranging collection of music from different cultures, different historical periods, different groups of players, different musical styles and genres, to inspire and inform children's music-making and performance.

Introductory stimulus is important in most music sessions, to encourage enthusiastic engagement and to empower children to respond with feeling, as much when teaching initial aspects of composition as when motivating a higher standard of playing and performing. Every listening activity requires some input, for instance, to teach children to focus, and help them to know exactly what to listen for. No artistic activity takes place in a vacuum. An image of the countryside might be a starting point for listening to Beethoven's *Pastoral Symphony*. Listening to a Hip Hop recording could provide a suitable stimulus for a small group to develop their own rap about a specific subject. A group of children in charge of the tape recorder on a class trip can result in an interesting tape of sounds to listen to on return to the classroom. A simple story told to children can be enhanced by musical sounds, such as *Peace at Last* by Jill Murphy; similar favourites can provide stimulus for younger children's sound-making.

Specific skills and techniques

Singing is perhaps the key to musical development, and requires the minimum of resources. Even without a confident teacher, children can sing a range of songs accompanied by tape recordings, now readily available, although live accompaniment may be preferable. Teacher and learner exploring together is a highly successful mode of learning, as there is no one method for developing musical understanding. Some schools still manage to employ instrumental teachers, who work with small groups towards a level of instrumental skill. This is invaluable, if expensive, and has diminished somewhat as a resource in schools (Cleave and Dust, 1989). Children who have instrumental skills can share their expertise with others, through performance and ensemble work. This in itself provides them with further experiences of music.

A developed listening skill is important for every aspect of learning. A child's levels of concentration are believed to be enhanced through listening to music and it has been found in recent research that children learn faster when listening to music (Edwards, 1996). This should be understood with caution but suffice to say that a variety of skills and knowledge in and about music can be highly beneficial to a child's learning of basic literacy, numeracy and scientific understanding. (This is explored further in Chapter 7.) Through a rich music education children can be encouraged to be sensitive to sounds in their environment and be able to create their own sounds, if they have learned from their teachers how to listen carefully.

Case Study 2

A West Country primary school with no music specialist took steps to provide each class teacher with a tape recorder and some prerecorded and blank tapes. Each teacher used the resources in a different way, according to the stage of development of the children. In the reception class, the tape recorder played music as a signal, when it was time to stop work and clear up. Children were not encouraged to hear music as a background to activity but rather as a signal to listen to carefully. Children cleared up quietly, as they listened and responded to the music. The teacher commented on how the children responded differently, depending on the music played and the children's mood. In a Year 5 class, the teacher recorded pieces of music that small groups of children had created. Children could then label, store and use it as appropriate for themselves. The tape recorder became a basic teaching tool, used for: recording children reading for expression; small groups working together to make 'radio programmes'; or creating a record of a particularly successful performance.

Time for reflection

Music occurs within a set time. It is therefore essential to allow time for children to reflect on their performances and compositions, if possible using a tape recorder. Discussion about musical performances and compositions is a valuable element in developing musical vocabulary and musical understanding.

Composition in music is similar to some approaches to creative writing, in that both employ a drafting process. Children need help in developing words to describe music as they explore the variety of sounds in their environment. Revisiting compositions, discussing them in groups, and critically evaluating their own and others' work, are all important aspects of pupils' musical development. Critical analysis of initial simple sound compositions leads to enhanced quality of future performances. Teachers need to allow time for reflection on musical achievements as it is this aspect which serves to consolidate learning, both in music and in speaking and listening *per se*.

Presentation of work

Performances of music are important and can be organised in a variety of different contexts and groupings. Small groups of pupils performing to the whole class can receive positive criticism from their peers, which enhances their capacity for listening. It is important to provide a range of different performance opportunities as this process can be frightening for children. Children who have many different opportunities in which to perform, the classroom, the school hall, outside, in a community hall, in a church, in a theatre, can build confidence and quality in performance. It is also valuable to ensure that children's own compositions are presented in some way. These could be performed live or recorded.

Summary

The musical elements described earlier need to be taught, revised, refined and continually revisited for children really to understand them, and to use the terms confidently in musical appreciation and music-making. Teacher and learner can together explore pieces of music, developing their language for describing it both in terms of musical elements and also in terms of the feelings it inspires and the structures that it employs. By providing children with a broad music education we are helping them personally to interpret the musical experiences they will encounter in life, and facilitating the sharing of the vast variety of music present in our culture.

Children's development of musical understanding is likely to be heavily influenced by the specialist or non-specialist music teacher's most valuable attribute: enthusiasm. There is so much music in our world to listen to and produce that the process can be as exciting for the teacher as it is for the children.

References

BEST, D. (1992) *The Rationality of Feeling: Understanding the Arts in Education*, London: Falmer Press.

BRITTEN, B. and HOLST, I. (1968) *The Wonderful World of Music*, London: Macdonald.

BROUGHTON, S., ELLINGHAM, M., MUDDYMAN, D., TRILLO, R. and BURTON, K. (1994) *The Rough Guide to World Music*, London: Rough Guides.

CLEAVE, S. and DUST, K. (1989) *A Sound Start: The Schools' Instrumental Music Service*, Windsor: NFER-Nelson.

DEPARTMENT OF EDUCATION AND SCIENCE (DES) (1991) *National Curriculum Music Working Group Interim Report*, London: HMSO.

DES (1992) *National Curriculum for Music*, London: HMSO.

DIAGRAM GROUP (1976) *Musical Instruments of the World*, New York: Facts of File Inc.

EDWARDS, R. (1996) 'Children learn faster to the sound of music', *New Scientist* **150**(2030), p. 6.

EISNER, E. (1982) *Cognition and the Curriculum*, Harlow: Longman.

ELLIOT, D. J. (1989) 'Key concepts in multicultural music education', *International Journal of Music Education* **13**, pp. 11–18.

LOWENFELD, M. (1987) 'Play in Childhood', in ABBS, P. (ed.), *Living Powers*, London: Falmer Press.

MURPHY, J. *Peace at Last*, London: Macmillan.

OEHRLE, E. (1996) 'Intercultural education through music: towards a culture of tolerance', *British Journal of Music Education* **13**(2), pp. 95–100.

SHEPHERD, J. and WICKE, P. (1997) *Music and Cultural Theory*, Malden: Polity Press.

SWANWICK, K. (1994) *Musical Knowledge: intuition, analysis and music education*, London: Routledge.

TARR, J. (1996) 'Arts Education: a process approach to the development of pedagogy', *British Journal of In-service Education*, **22**(3), pp. 293–308.

TIPPETT, M. (1974) *Moving into Aquarius*, London: Paladin.

Chapter 4

Talking with children about art

Gloria Callaway and Mary Kear

Case Study 1

A group of 10-year-old British children study a large reproduction of a Gauguin painting, *When Will You Marry Me?*, painted in Tahiti in 1892.[1]

D: She's got a blend of green on her face.

T: But you can't notice this green a lot, it's just on the nose, a white shading.

D: I think it's a type of shade but she [sic] might not have had the proper colour – she's gone to a darker brown for shade on her hair, and green for shade there.

S: Over here it's blue and yellow – green – he'd used green over here but he'd mixed blue and yellow over there . . . he might have used a black colour or used double the same colour . . . I know, he put green and then he just kept putting . . . kept putting some more green, kept putting it on.

Later, looking at Van Gogh's *Self Portrait with Grey Hat*, they comment:

N: If you looked at this from a few metres away this would look like a proper painting, but when you come in you see that it's just lines and dots; from over there, it is a proper painting, it looks like it hasn't been done with lines and dots.

D: If you didn't see that (signature), you would know it was Van Gogh; I saw one before and when he painted he just squidged and streaked.

S: It starts in the middle, then it goes in all directions, like a circle, like the wind.

D: I know, maybe he's standing in front of the world.

Reflection 1

What knowledge do these children each have about art? How can you tell?

If you were their teacher, what would you think they needed to learn next?

How would you set about teaching them more about painting and artists?

Teaching about art involves talking. We talk with children about their practical work, or image-making: setting tasks, instructing, advising and assessing. We talk with children about the work of artists, and help them appreciate the different colours, textures, forms or compositions used. The hard part seems to be putting these two aspects together, so that children's growing knowledge and understanding of techniques and skills influences their appreciation of artists' work, which in turn helps them to make art in a more competent, confident and expressive way.

In this chapter we consider talking about children's and artists' work, and offer pointers as to how to link the work of artists to children's own practical art-making in schools. We also consider how not talking (as well as listening) might play a vital role in the teacher's approach to the study of art and artists in the classroom. As teachers, we are encouraged to think critically about the purpose and structure of the questions we ask and the comments we make. We consider the profile we adopt in discussions, and assess children's success in carrying out tasks we set, partly through reflections on the clarity and effectiveness of our introduction, instruction, interventions and demonstrations during the process.

We are all 'consumers' and 'producers' of language. Within primary education, reports such as those by Plowden (1967), Cockroft (1982) and Kingman (1988) encouraged us to examine and improve our own and the children's language until, as a profession, many of us feel comfortable with how language and learning fuel each other, and how, as teachers, we can best facilitate learning. Talking about art and artists has not been subject to the same scrutiny, even in the comprehensive and influential Calouste-Gulbenkian Foundation's Report (1982). Uncertainty in talking about the arts is professed by teachers and students on a regular basis within our hearing. Yet in teaching mathematics, reading and writing, problem-solving through exploration and discussion is a successful strategy, employed by the same skilled teachers who are nervous about discussing art and artists.

> ❝ *If what distinguishes a subject is its distinctive conventions of thought and particular conceptions of phenomena, the task for teachers is to communicate those conventions and conceptions as useful, albeit provisional, ways of understanding the world. . . . At the centre of a genre or discourse mode is a shared way of living and the common understandings that go with it.*
>
> (Barnes and Sheeran, 1992, p. 93)

Many teachers who know how to use particular tools and techniques have little problem in talking about the processes in art, demonstrating how to use equipment or encouraging children to acquire the skills of making. But we tend to opt out of evaluating artworks, by children or by artists, being steeped in the notion that to criticise is inappropriate, and might shatter the confidence of the child. Engaging in talk about the nature of the experience, the quality of the outcome, eliciting comments on responses and feelings and making evaluations is difficult. We need to find ways of identifying and communicating conventions and conceptions which are appropriate for the children we teach.

Within the National Curriculum orders, there is an implicit recognition of the role of discourse within visual art education, through the use of words such as *review*, *describe*, *explain*, *reflect on*. In practical and potentially expressive art sessions, we are required to teach as well as *give experience*, which implies both instruction and demonstration by the teacher. Children *modify their work*, under the guidance of a more able other. The teacher's skill lies in identifying the current level of achievement, and facilitating the child's next steps, through constructive criticism during the process of making or coming to an understanding. For the teacher, congratulation and appreciation of today's efforts are formulated into tomorrow's goals.

It can be argued that children demonstrate their understanding of the artistic process and the thinking that surrounds it through the shapes, forms and textures they achieve as a result of their physical and intellectual interactions with media. On occasion, this seems neither to require, nor automatically to generate, spoken language. As teachers, we may need to learn how to see the evidence, rather than insist on verbal exposition of an essentially visual experience. Art is *per se* a unique and independent form of expression and communication. It affords opportunities to explore, interpret and represent a range of ideas with a rich vocabulary of its own, for which spoken language would be an inadequate alternative. Both younger and older primary pupils are capable of deploying a visual/graphic repertoire which can well outstrip their ability to express themselves in written or spoken language.

 The power of words constitutes a principal reason that most children come to favor them rather than drawing as a means of self-expression.

(Gardner, 1980, p. 151)

The culture in which we live and teach is dominated by the written word. Even in practical art sessions, the tendency is for talk to dominate 60 per cent of the time, and the teacher's talk for 60 per cent of that time (Edwards and Mercer, 1987, 25). In rooms where we teach primary children, language is paramount. It is the main instrument for communication, through instruction, discussion, explanation and testing. The primary class teacher works hard to facilitate high levels of interaction, but we may ask how well we are equipped to engage in discourse which is appropriate to the subject in hand, to establish further understanding about and around it.

Research (Tickle, 1996; Holt, 1989) indicates that there is an almost universal uncertainty, even with experienced art specialists, around talking to children about art and artists. Experience suggests that when children purposefully engage with artists' work, through appropriately challenging tasks and discussion linked with their own practical work, both their appreciation of artists' work and their own ability to make art measurably improve. In framing that discussion, selecting particular examples and setting tasks, is it appropriate to use the same sort of language as when, for instance, we talk about science, mathematics or history?

> *Being able to use the genre appropriate to the curricular activity in progress may be as important a part of being communicatively confident as is being able to use the appropriate social register. . . . Are the language and thought patterns of specialised subjects somehow inextricably interwoven?*
>
> (Norman, 1992, p. 293)

We may, therefore, need to think beyond the terminology associated with 'art', and to reflect more on the real significance of that terminology, and how it represents concepts which can be understood at different levels of complexity according to the age, experience and education of the pupil. The question Norman poses is one you may debate with colleagues in terms of your own subject or media specialism.

Visual symbols, and the graphic representation of ideas and responses to experience, offer modes of learning, expression and communication. Nonetheless, to effect progression, the teacher needs to access children's thinking, and to do so, one of the major tools available is the ability to reflect on their language and spoken responses.

Think back to the children in the case study. Despite her theoretical knowledge of the 'colour wheel', which she could draw unaided, child S concludes that to make darker green, Gauguin 'kept putting more on'. You do not need to be an oil painter to understand that putting more of the same paint on the canvas is unlikely to change the colour itself. So the ability to recite a particular formula did not in this case give her any insight into the way the artist worked. The teacher worked with the class on mixing pigments and making a range of colours. Once she had tried this, child S realised that Gauguin had, in fact, added more blue, and thus achieved the light and shade effects they were talking about.

The description by these children of Van Gogh's painterly technique, and the significance of brushstrokes, suggests a critical but perhaps untutored approach, searching for appropriate ways of describing what interested and engaged them about the paintings. These snatches of talk indicate that these children were on the point of realising that there were major things in common between these two artists, Van Gogh and Gauguin, as you may have already concluded. Teachers use information from discussions such as this to plan for progression, identifying children's potential from information gleaned about their current levels of understanding.

Carefully considered discourse with and between pupils helps to promote their understanding of the different facets and nuances of the spoken and written word, to establish order, and to generate purposeful activity and positive learning. One of a primary teacher's greatest assets is the ability to initiate and facilitate discussion, establishing clear joint understandings, pitching questions and comments at the right level, adopting 'inclusive' approaches which value each child's contribution, providing relevant information at relevant times, and helping children progress from initial hesitancy to confident articulation of knowledge gained and concepts grasped.

All of these abilities come into play in art sessions, during both practical work and in teaching about art and artists. The next section addresses Attainment Target 2 in the National Curriculum: 'Knowledge and Understanding'. In particular, we consider questions, and ways of questioning. For ease of reference, the discussion is about paintings, although the issues addressed will apply equally to drawing, ceramics, print or sculpture. Later, we discuss issues related to talking to children about their own artwork.

Talking about art and artists

Not every primary teacher can be an art historian, but the National Curriculum requires primary teachers to teach children about art and artists. Benefits for the teacher include the excuse to browse through enticing books and visit galleries in preparation for any topic or project, and the fact that personal preferences and knowledge can be exploited and developed through the process of selection from the literally millions of examples available to use with children. This said, it is perhaps appropriate to note one of the conclusions of a recent research project.

Teachers in Key Stage 2 need to broaden the range of artists and designers they use . . . beyond the present over-emphasis upon the use of the work of the Impressionist and Post-Impressionist painters and to consider how to use such work, other than as source material for the simple imitation, by children, of the work of the artists chosen for study. (Clement and Jones, 1996, p. 64)

This applies equally to teachers of early years pupils, and it is hoped that, in carrying out some of the suggested enquiry tasks in this chapter, you may choose to select artists' work which broadens and extends your own knowledge of art and artists. We can all, probably, say with accuracy, 'I know what I like', but as primary generalist and specialist teachers we need to take it further. After all, we can hardly opt out of teaching the Romans, because we only like the Egyptians and the Victorians.

In initiating discussion with children about a painting, the safe course is to ask straightforward questions about the content, such as '*what can you see?*', the medium, '*what colours are there?*', and an initial response, typically '*how does it make you feel?*' They are comfortable, familiar questions, which children expect, and which establish a mutual understanding: children answer questions, then the teacher provides information. We consider the merits of each question in turn, as a way of examining how questioning can encourage, or may discourage, children's engagement with a painting.

What can you see in the painting?

The response is likely to be brief, one-word lists of items, such as the people, details of the landscape, room, objects or buildings. Children may try to seek out something no-one has mentioned yet, to add to the list: the naming of parts. The question presupposes that there are items to be seen and catalogued, searched out and named, and the child is instantly focused on this way of thinking about and responding to the work. The teacher needs to beware promoting a 'guessing game' (Edwards and Mercer, 1987, p. 31), but should instead use the question to focus children's attention on the image in front of them. If there are no 'items' (for instance in some works of Vasarely, Mondrian or Bridget Riley), consider what the response would be.

Usually, a painting is the result of careful decisions about colours, textures and items: which to put in or leave out, where to place elements within a given frame, and, later, whether or not the work is finished. The artist may well have moved parts of the picture around in the process of painting it, or changed colours, or made a mistake and decided to keep it in. The finished painting may have little to do with the literal appearance of its subject, a person, a landscape or an arrangement of objects ('still life'). It is simply a series of 'two-dimensional' marks on a surface; subjects are shown as seen by the artist, a unique response to stimulus.

Marks are deliberately placed in a particular composition, just as we might choose items of clothing to wear together because we like the total effect. A twist of a scarf, a change of tie, the addition of a piece of jewellery will each add something to the overall effect. We may not wish our friends to know how long we spent fiddling with the components; when we are ready, we want everything 'just right'. In the same way, for most artists, the decision-making stages of the process are between them and the canvas, not something the viewer needs to know about. However, for children, understanding that there has been a process, that decisions have been made and preliminary work done, is important if they are also to engage in the challenging occupation of making their own art.

We often hear that there is 'no right or wrong' in art, a perhaps debatable point. To assert that there is a white rabbit in a painting made entirely of yellow squares is clearly inaccurate. On the other hand, there may be an infinite number of ways of being 'right', for instance in responding to a work of art in a negative, positive or even disinterested way, or all at the same time, for different reasons. If you state that the yellow painting reminds you of a white rabbit, no-one can say it does not, although you might not find it easy to explain convincingly. In that sense, there is no 'right' response, just as the good teacher of art does not impose solutions and products on pupils for practical tasks, but helps them to work individually and creatively towards a personal art product.

Enquiry task 1

Look at a familiar representational painting, perhaps a 'still life'. List what you see in the painting. You may notice items, objects or details you had not previously realised were there. Now look at another, less familiar painting, and respond to these questions.
- What is in the foreground of the painting?
- What is in the background?
- How did the artist help you to know which is which?
- What most draws your attention in the picture?
- Does your eye travel from one thing to another?
- Are there any tricks the artist has used to make you look from one thing to another in the painting?
- Consider why the artist included these items, and only these items, in the painting.

Now, look at a painting which is not representational but which is made up of colours and shapes. Try not to think about whether or not it reminds you of anything, and respond to these questions.

- What is the most notable feature of the painting?
- Is there a shape which is repeated – do you notice any sort of pattern?
- Are the shapes in the painting outlined in any way, or are they placed directly adjacent to each other?
- Do some areas appear closer to you than others?
- Is there in any sense a 'background' and 'foreground'?

Think of other questions you could use with children to help them appreciate:
- the overall composition of the work;
- the relationship between the objects etc. depicted;
- the information conveyed in the painting.

What colours do you see in the painting?

It is likely that a further list is generated, combined with items: blue horses, green trees, red sky. For a 'pure abstract' work, comprising only colours and shapes, responses may be about familiar shapes: a blue square, a black line, a white triangle. Such a list is fairly quickly exhausted, even with a quite complex composition. The tendency, even for older children, is to reply with basic colour names, primaries and secondaries, rather than to look closely at the range of reds, blues or oranges that might be there. The teacher should help them to look more perceptively.

Most paintings use a 'limited palette': the artist selects which range of colours, where, and in what proportions will best suit the overall intentions of the work. So, children's responses to the question above may well be confined to three or four colours, of which there may be many shades and tones. For the viewer, some will usually be dominant and some less dominant. A small streak of red within an otherwise mainly blue and green picture will be very obvious. Some of Van Gogh's *Sunflower* paintings have a thin line of blue to denote where the table surface finishes, and his signature is also in blue. This touch of blue highlights the yellows, oranges and greens elsewhere on the canvas. Take it away and the whole colour balance is changed. Try covering up one of the colours in a painting you know, and see how it changes the overall colour composition. It is difficult to describe the effect, but most viewers will notice a change, including children. Look at some abstract work which uses geometric composition, for instance Mondrian's *Composition*, Malevich's *Suprematism*, Rothko's *Untitled* or Bomberg's *The Mud Bath*. Consider how the shapes or areas within it are defined. Are different colours placed next to each other, or has the artist gradually 'shaded' areas? How do some artists use lines together with areas of colour? Cover part of one of these pictures and see how the balance of the composition changes.

Some artists have tried to give all colours equal 'value' within a painting, which was one of the ways in which 'Op-art' paintings (short for 'optical art') in the sixties achieved their illusions of movement. The juxtaposition of strong colours of similar tones means that the whole area of the canvas is alive with colour, which really seems to move. Bridget Riley and Vasarely are among the most well-known artists who worked in the Pop-art tradition. Children can compare and contrast the different ways these artists used colour with the approaches used by the artists mentioned above.

Another way of considering colour is to look at how one colour, for instance yellow, is used by different artists from a range of 'schools'. Putting together an abstract painting such as Albers' yellow *Homage to the Square*, Van Gogh's *Sunflowers*, and another painting with dominant yellows, such as Klee's *Senecio* or Gainsborough's *Mr and Mrs Andrews*, can lead children into comparisons and contrasts of colour and colour use, which will highlight their appreciation of and ability to see nuances within familiar hues, and to identify aspects of style, composition and genre.

Colour can be used to create a sensation of movement, for instance in water. Turner, Hodler and David Hockney have respectively attempted to depict in static, two-dimensional paint the force of the sea, the tranquil surface of a lake or the splash of water in a swimming pool. In *Snowstorm: Steamboat off a Harbour's Mouth*, Turner creates enormous, dramatic and exciting waves with swirls of grey, brown and yellow, while Hodler's almost symmetrical patterns in shades of blue, white and peach depict gentle ripples in his painting of *Lake Thun*. David Hockney's *A Bigger Splash* uses fine, lively, white brushstrokes against a blue background, to describe the impact of a diver on the previously calm surface of a pool. Each painting invites us to look around the surface of the picture to appreciate the effects of that powerful element, water, in different settings. The paint stays still, but the artists make it almost seem to move, in an entirely different way from Bridget Riley's use of colour to depict movement in *Cataract 3* and other works.

Artists often challenge our conventional views of the world around us. Asked 'what colour is the sea?', most of us would respond 'blue'. Yet, Klein's *YKB*, which is pure blue, looks less like water than any of the paintings mentioned above. Even a cursory search through books of art and photographs to do with the sea will reveal that in fact it is only blue in certain circumstances, and that many painters have completely eschewed blue pigment when depicting it, or included so many other colours that the blue is certainly not the dominant or central colour of the painting, as with Turner's work and Spillaert's *Moonlit Beach*. Such paintings demonstrate which colours attract the artists; to examine this work helps children to see that pre-mixed blue is about as useful to describe the sea as pre-mixed pink is to describe the skin of even the blondest anglo-saxon.

Asking children to name or count items, list colours, and note detail to the exclusion of the whole, can constitute a test, in that the teacher knows the answers and the children are trying to guess what she wants to hear, to get it right. While it is unarguable that any items which may be depicted, and the colours that are used are important, the fact is that it is a painting. It is first and foremost the sum of its parts, rather than a haphazard amalgam of colour and canvas.

Children need time and space to take in the colours and the composition of the painting as a whole, like tasting good food, to relish the experience, rather than to have to work out the ingredients and how hot the oven was for how long. Such curiosity is probably best left unsatisfied for the time being. Meanwhile, the teacher has provided 'visual scaffolding', in carefully choosing appropriate visual stimulus to promote intense appreciation of colour, composition and style, rather than being dependent on words to explain. In fact, there is no obvious way of teaching children about colour and texture and composition without such visual scaffolding, with or without accompanying verbal discourse.

Enquiry task 2

Use the same paintings as in the previous task. First, look carefully at the one you know best. Then close your eyes, and think about which colour you remember as being most dominant, and the second most dominant. Then, open your eyes and look again.
- Are the same colours dominant?
- Are these colours the ones that cover most of the canvas?

If not, try to think why it was that you remembered those particular colours. Perhaps they are in the foreground. Background colours, which may take up more space on the canvas, could have been intended to 'show up' the colours of other items.
- Look at the background of the painting.
- Why do you think the artist chose that colour or range of colours?
- Can you see the same colour/s anywhere else in the painting?
- Has the artist used different shades and tones for different reasons?

Try out similar questions with children, to help them appreciate:
- the range of colours used (and those not present);
- the different colours in, for example, a person's skin, a tree, or a shadow;
- the way colour is used for different purposes within the painting.

How does the painting make you feel?

There is often an association made between colour and 'mood', although paintings dominated by so-called 'warm' colours like yellow and red, are not necessarily 'happy', any more than muted or 'cold' colours are used only to depict sombre subjects. Picasso's *Weeping Woman* is a very powerful expression of grief in bright reds, yellows and greens, and Rouault uses vibrant colours to depict scenes which are, to him, of deep religious significance. On the other hand, the two most famous smiles in Western art, Leonardo da Vinci's *Mona Lisa* and Franz Hals' *Laughing Cavalier* are painted using a range of relatively dark colours, and Lowry celebrates aspects of ordinary people's lives in quite dull, sometimes rather muddy colours. We should beware of encouraging children to make simplistic connections between colours and moods, just as we should avoid coming to dangerous conclusions about their emotional state because of the colours *they* choose when making art.

Seemingly straightforward discussions about content and colour in paintings can clearly trigger in-depth, meaningful visual appreciation and purposeful discussion of art and artists. This third, often posed question, is rather more problematic, in that there would seem to be a limited number of words a child can use in response, beyond the basic list of sad, happy, cold, hot, etc. Of course, children might have particularly interesting things to say about examples of Op-art, which can in some cases produce a physical reaction. However, we would question the supposition, implicit in the question 'how does it make you feel?', that everyone has an *emotional* response when viewing a work of art. Such a response may be simply absent, but in any case it is rarely instant, and is almost always difficult to articulate. It can be said with some certainty that the artist was, while making it, trying to communicate through the painting, but most adults find it quite hard to find examples of paintings which really promote strong, describable emotions.

The authors have asked this of numerous students (and children), and come to the conclusion that it first provokes blank looks, bemused expressions and, more often than not, some laughter with the realisation that the question is almost impossible to answer in almost every case. What was the artist trying to 'say'? Not always : 'I want you to be sad, happy, angry or content' with this picture. Indeed, some paintings which we find familiar and comfortable, for instance Monet's and Seurat's, were quite shocking and challenging in their day.

Reflection 2

Look again at one of your paintings. Try to describe how it makes you feel.

A painting can be viewed or dismissed at a glance; it can be tempting to allow initial responses to guide subsequent actions, and not to persevere as

Reflection 3

Select three paintings, originals in a gallery if possible, or good reproductions. Make yourself comfortable, and spend at least three to five minutes just looking at each. Your mind may be blank, or you may be actively searching the picture for detail. This does not matter. What matters is that you spend overall some ten minutes absorbing the images. Then, stand so that at least two of them are in your line of vision, and look from one to the other, noting perhaps how they differ, and how they might be similar. Could you say, confidently, what it was about these pictures that made you choose them? Can you articulate similarities and differences in the paintings?

we might with a book, a film or a piece of music. Children may fare better with silence: a chance to let their eyes wander around the picture, to have time to establish a relationship with the work, and, by doing so, with the artist.

What do children see when they look at a painting?

This is probably easier than simply trying to articulate verbal responses to a painting which is communicating to you visually. Having tried the reflections above yourself, you might like to try the same with a group of children. You might even use an egg-timer to denote the period during which no verbal response is required (or allowed), to reinforce the idea that pictures are for looking at, as music is for listening to: verbal responses, descriptions, analysis come later. Sometimes, both teachers and children need to just look, free from pressure, thus avoiding the traditional roles sceptically described as follows.

 Pupils and teacher seem to spend much of their time playing the roles of competitors and question master [sic] *in an ill-defined, hastily conceived quiz.*

(Edwards and Mercer, 1987, p. 29)

The teacher's ability to effect purposeful talk or non-talk is dependent largely on the degree of 'match' achieved for the different ages and ability levels within the class, through careful assessment of children's needs and potential, recognition of the value of previous experience, and the setting of suitably challenging but achievable tasks. What often goes unremarked, unappreciated, unnoticed, is how often communication occurs through and during silence, non-verbal sound, sight, reading, writing, making and 'just looking', when the teacher recognises the value of wordless engagement with an experience, a problem or task. Here, the skill is in not intervening or interrupting. Silence in the classroom is not always a sign of oppression and rigid discipline, as we are reminded when children say to each other, 'Be quiet, I'm drawing!'

Case Study 2

The same three children discuss *Tea Time*, a painting by Marie Braquemond.[2] They first just look, saying nothing for a few minutes. Then, they quietly focus on colours, partly because they had tried to create colours of their own in paint the day before. They identify green, blue, bluish white, light blue, peach, black, shades, a lot of yellow. There is familiarity in this, but subsequent talk evidences their fascination with 'tricks of the trade', how the artist had achieved certain effects through skilled application of pigments.

T: It looks windy because it's like the paint's streaking in one direction.
S: It's streaking! It's got like pale dots in it. It looks like the colours are trying to push and get in the way – push away and push.
D: A windy blowing effect – but if it was windy, her hat would have keeled. It's a windy blowing effect, but it's not windy.

T points to a red brushstroke in the top left-hand corner of the painting, denoting a small house in the distance, the only red in an otherwise fairly muted painting.

D: There's a bit of red there; everything else is green and white and that stuff, and that little piece of red just there and nobody else would notice it; it just comes right out.
T: The house is up there and goes down like that and there's sort of water but because there's so much detail there, there's not so much over there and – like – a red would notice more.

Enquiry task 3

Find evidence in the way the children talked of the different ways in which they now look at paintings. Can you think how their own practical work might have influenced their discussion?

The children had time to look at the work, and they picked up each others' comments and added to them, such as the idea that the red was to draw your attention to that part of the painting. The logic they brought to the discussion means that the artist's way of working was important to them, partly since they had also been preoccupied with getting the right effect in their own practical work. That the woman was reading a book and drinking tea went unremarked, until they later looked at Mary Cassat's *Woman Sewing* and Gwen John's *The Precious Book*, and noticed similarities in composition.

There is sometimes a dilemma about whether or not to provide information about a painting before discussion. What information do children need about, say, a painting? As with all such questions in education, the answer begins, 'it depends . . .', on what they know, what they see and what they want to know. The discerning teacher takes cues from initial responses. When discourse is appropriate, the 'I wonder . . .' statement is a useful starting point, as in 'I wonder what the artist was thinking about when doing this picture', 'I wonder if the artist got the picture right first go', 'I wonder where the artist was when this picture was made.' Initial questions or 'I wonder . . .' statements need to be carefully formulated to give the children maximum scope for demonstrating and articulating their current levels of understanding and appreciation.

Giving 'input' about the artists may or may not be helpful at the outset. Showing a series of works by the same artist, first individually and then together, will undoubtedly help children to identify aspects of the artist's style. Showing a range of pictures by several artists will introduce other elements into the discussion, as with the yellow pictures mentioned earlier. Child A, who said Van Gogh 'squidged and squeezed' the paint, later looked at Vlaminck and other 'squidgers', and was able further to refine his appreciation of how Van Gogh worked, and who else did similar work. He had started to understand what the term 'school of art' means.

A previous chapter in this book is devoted to the role of narrative in the arts. Storytelling is yet another area of expertise for the primary teacher, which includes, but is not confined to, reading literature. Narrative is also a tool for learning about scientific ideas, such as how a bulb lights or a gas forms or a seed grows. History is essentially the story of how people and places grow and adapt according to circumstances. Through narrative, the teacher brings alive what is to be taught in the classroom. This is as true in visual arts education as other curricular areas, and is here considered because of how it can help teachers with the issue of presenting ideas and information about art and artists in an accessible way.

In reading stories and poems to children, we occasionally discuss the process through which the writer has developed characters, or how the immediate environment influenced the choice of location for the story, for example in such classics as *Wind in the Willows* or *Alice* books. *Peter Pan* was set in Kensington Gardens where the author, J.M. Barrie, went often with the boys to whom he told the story, and Beatrix Potter lived next to Peter Rabbit's garden. This sense of time and place is also important to the creators of visual art: it is most unlikely that Monet would have painted those water-lilies in that garden if he had not planted them there himself, or that Turner's seas would have looked the same if he lived in California. Artists often draw inspiration from their immediate surroundings and personal experiences. Turner was even said to have strapped himself to the mast of a ship in a storm in order to experience what he later depicted in his painting *Snowstorm: Steamboat off a Harbour's Mouth*, and it is probably true that Hokusai had experience of being in a boat in a storm before creating the wonderful *Great Wave* woodcut. We need not go to these lengths to inspire children, but we do need to give them first-hand experiences of an appropriate kind. The imagination needs food.

Artists also focus on the detail and richness of their domestic surroundings, as Van Gogh did when painting his bedroom, or Berthe Morisot painting her sister by the cradle. Children's immediate, familiar and comfortable surroundings can also provide them with inspiration, especially when they notice that many real artists took similar subject matter for their work, as did the children looking at the paintings of Marie Bracquemond, Cassatt and Gwen John. Each of these artists has a fascinating biography, and to tell the stories of the artists with whose paintings the children have become familiar makes them real to the children, as well as providing good examples of biography or autobiography as genres. Rembrandt, Van Gogh and Hogarth all painted many self-portraits which themselves tell fascinating stories, which children can piece together through looking at them. After all, they are asked to depict themselves at regular intervals throughout their school careers, and will have at least this in common with 'Great Masters', and their female counterparts.

Although the artist will generally wish to be considered in the light of the most recent work, to help children understand the process of creativity it is vital to consider the inspiration behind the work, which may be economic or visual. Just as Dickens had to get chapter after chapter ready and finished to strict publishing deadlines for his serial novels, artists who work to commission have briefs to follow in a given time. Published artists' sketchbooks can be borrowed from the local library for children to see how works of art are developed, through sketches, research, sometimes trial and error, through to completed paintings. Such processes are fascinating, and familiar to children who know how long it takes to write a story or make a painting, and how many compromises have to be made on the way.

In working with children and art, there are many positive and useful starting points to be taken from other work in hand in the classroom. While the art session will focus on visual art, the work will enhance the way children 'read' other visual images, help them towards an understanding of the significance of framing, composition, choice of viewpoint, and devices used, such as colour, brushstrokes, light and shade, as well as the subject and content of the work. Thus, through providing suitable examples to compare and contrast, and promoting appropriate discourse, the teacher can help children better to see the world around them, as well as experiencing how others see and record, and comment on the world around them at particular times and in particular places, in history and now.

Bruner (1983) coined the term 'handover', to describe how children:

 [. . .] come to take control of the process [language] for themselves. Language learners and craft apprentices become masters of the art. . . . It is here that we find one of the most problematical aspects of formal education.

(Edwards and Mercer, 1987, p. 23)

As teachers we know well that teaching something does not necessarily imply that our pupils have learned or understood, let alone that we have achieved 'handover'. In the next section of this chapter, a technique is described which, appropriately used, can help further the teacher's understandings of pupils' grasp of ideas and terminology within the genre of visual art, through initiating a particular form of discourse through questioning. This in turn helps the teacher decide how best to take children's knowledge and understanding on to a further stage.

Construct elicitation technique

Later work with the children we met above, and some of their classmates, was based on 'construct elicitation technique', a method originated by Kelly (1963), and used to examine children's perceptions of television (Eke and Croll, 1992).

 In appraising a particular visual image, both similarity and familiarity will affect how aspects such as shape, pattern, colour or subject matter are organised and responded to. . . . Where there are no constructs, no adequate perception or understanding can be achieved. (Osbourn, 1989, p. 323)

Here, the technique helped the teacher to elicit and identify what constructs these children had, that is, what they could see when they looked at paintings. They were shown reproductions of paintings of people, three at a time, and asked to identify something similar about two of them which was different from the third. Then, one painting was removed and replaced with a fourth, and the same question was posed. This was repeated until they had run out of ways of describing similarities and differences, usually after some ten or fifteen paintings had been presented. The children were not told what to look for, so their responses gave clues as to what they were able to discern for themselves in the paintings.

Over time, doing similar exercises with different paintings, including Japanese, Indian and African artists and subjects, and in between learning how to mix and apply paint for themselves, their comments became increasingly detailed. For example, while they began with comments such as 'two are women, one's a man', later comments were much more sophisticated, such as 'those two have thin paint and lots of detail, but the other one is more sketchy and you can't see the features'. An analysis of children's comments revealed their concern with six areas, as follows:

■ *content*: appearance, activity, the setting, the character or feelings of the subjects, cultural background;
■ *style*: amount of detail, use of colour, bold or tentative lines, thick or thin paint or brushes;
■ *media*: pencil sketches, paintings, charcoal, mixed paint and drawing media;
■ *composition*: whole figure, head and shoulders or three-quarter length depicted; profile or full face; central or not in the frame; amount of background;
■ *period*: 'Victorian' or 'old fashioned' were used indiscriminately to describe pictures which were not 'modern', a term which tended to be applied to 'abstract' or brightly coloured, bold work;
■ *opinions*: these were few; 'better' clearly meant more detailed or 'realistic' work; they were not impressed with anything 'too scribbly', or with 'boring' colours.

Even if it is acquired in less of a systematic fashion, data like this can help the teacher to decide where to pitch tasks and discussions, and the phrasing of 'I wonder' questions, to help children adopt a more enquiring and purposeful consideration of paintings. Work on this task seemed to help children's confidence in discussing other work, such as *Tea Time*, as described above. This technique may help you understand more about children's perceptions.

Enquiry task 4

Collect a series of reproductions of artists' work, with a common theme such as portraits, landscapes or still life. Postcards may be adequate, although good quality larger reproductions are best. Set them out three at a time for a small group to view. After a pause, ask them to say what is the same about two which is different from the third. Then, take away one and substitute with another, in turn. Note their comments, and later examine the data to see what types of responses they made. Do they fall into the categories above, or are they about different aspects of the work? What do the children's comments tell you about what they see when they look at visual images?

You may also use this data to help you assess how well children understand the concepts of the 'elements of art', as listed in the National Curriculum for Key Stages 1 and 2: '. . . visual and tactile qualities of pattern, texture, colour, line, tone, and shape, form and space' (Qualifications and Curriculum Authority, 1998, p. 15).

Talking about children's own work

Making connections between discussions of artists' work and children's own practical work may be facilitated if the teacher chooses examples of artists' work which link in both subject matter and medium with on-going class work. For instance, the work based on construct elicitation technique, described above, was linked to a series of lessons on portraits and portrait painting. This is also why the examples used in the group discussions were portraits of different types.

However, teaching the terms 'pattern', 'texture' and so on as vocabulary items will not necessarily help children's understandings. Look back at the excerpts of transcripts, and try to identify how they evidence children's appreciation of the 'elements of art'. Remember, although these children were later years primary, they had only just started to work in this way, and a similar level of understanding may well be possible with much younger children if they are given appropriate input, experience and opportunity.

Teachers' practice in primary schools has been influenced, even dominated, by socio-constructivist theories of learning, which stress the importance of teacher–pupil discourse. Consider the following brief exchange, as children in a classroom begin to paint.

Case Study 3

The children sit on the carpet as the teacher (Tr) gives out reminders about the work each group is to undertake in the afternoon. The art group is to continue with designing and painting posters for the library, using watercolour paintboxes. They organise their workspace, and sit in self-selected pairs. One of the children, P, needs some help, because he has not got quite what he wants in his design.

Tr: So look, P, this is your place and what you need is another piece of paper to do this, here.
P: I know what you mean – do this on another piece of paper.
Tr: Exactly. I couldn't have put it better myself.

The children work absorbed in their painting, and after a short time, the teacher revisits the group.

Reflection 4

Think through the evidence
there is in this brief account
of the teacher supporting, but
encouraging independence, in the
group. In what ways has the
teacher effected 'handover', and
what would be the next steps for
P to improve his understanding
and technical competence? Does
this account of classroom work
remind you in any way of the
previous group of children we
encountered? Think about what
information you derived from the
reported speech, and what you
learned from the description
of the child at work. What
significance is there in this
distinction?

P: I want to do it pink.

Tr: Pink? What colour is it like?

P: Red.

Tr: Yes, a bit like red. Now, how can you make that red look more like pink? What other colour can you see in the pink?

P: It's lighter.

Tr: Let's think about what lighter means, and how you can make the red lighter. Look at the sky.

P: It's blue.

Tr: What colour are the clouds?

P: White.

Tr: Exactly. Now, can you see where the clouds float across the sky, it looks lighter.

P mixes white paint, adds red bit by bit, until a sufficient quantity of the required shade of pink is achieved. He works thoroughly absorbed, looking intently at the mixing palette while filling his brush, and then at the paper as he paints. From time to time he looks at his work critically, his head pulled slightly further back to get a better view. Then he continues the process. He is at perfect ease with his materials and tools, handling the brush with dexterity to form the letter shapes, and controlling the paint expertly. Later, talking to a neighbour, P exclaims enthusiastically:

P: I started off with the white. I made pink!

Barnes (1976, p. 197) devised a simple model, assumed to be 'both idealised and very familiar', in relation to managing small group work in four stages: the focusing stage, the exploratory stage, the reorganising stage and the public stage, as also mentioned in Chapter 1. It may be helpful to consider the types of talk teachers use at different points in a practical art session.

Tr: Bring all your work over here. You won't need aprons, just brushes and newspaper. . . . Is this the right size brush for doing this? Shall we get another one?

Introductory talk is rarely 'discourse', in that the teacher usually talks to the children, introduces the context, sets the scene, recalls previous experience and learning and gives instructions on the set task or tasks to be completed by the children. It also communicates, implicitly or explicitly, the rationale for the task, organisational details such as access to resources, and behavioural expectations, for instance in terms of noise level, acceptable movement around the room, systems for asking for help and so on.

C: I done a grey, look.

Tr: The white's gone grey, has it? You might want to change your water. You need to make sure your brush is quite clean.

P: How do you make grey?

Tr: What sort of letters do you want? Are you going to do yours like C? Will you make them little or big? C, will you show P what you have done? Go and see if there is a book in the book corner with a border you like.

Once children have started work on set tasks, discourse is largely initiated by the teacher, based on observation of how children are progressing. She also notes signs and signals of potential problems and spots opportunities to stretch particular children's thinking a little further, through the practised routine of ensuring coverage of the class. This careful 'choreography' is often achieved through working with each group in turn, to stimulate, motivate and develop ideas, while regularly pausing to deal with the whole class, individuals or groups who have signalled the need for assistance, reassurance or information, sometimes given to an individual so others will overhear.

Tr: Now, everyone in the art group needs to start packing away, so remember to clean and stack the paintboxes, sort the brushes and fold up the newspaper. P and C will be doing the washing up today. Then get your work to show the rest of the class in sharing time.

During the final stages of a taught session, the teacher again uses organisational instruction, and facilitates the appropriate atmosphere within which children can assess, evaluate and reflect on their efforts under her guidance. The quality and value of this part of the session depends on the quality of previous interactions. The clearer the initial instructions, including the articulation of learning intentions for the children, the more focus can be achieved in evaluating the success of the task and the quality of learning achieved.

Tr: The art group has been working on library posters. Let's look quietly at the work before we talk about it. As you look, remember what the posters are for, and think about how effective these will be when they are finished and put up.

The nature of the discourse that a teacher promotes and generates in the classroom reflects the philosophy of teaching espoused. Within a social-constructivist approach, the aim would be to keep organisational and instructional talk to a minimum, in order to maximise potential for focused teaching. To pass on to the children as efficiently as possible, sometimes in whole-class settings, skills, such as mixing paints or doing good lettering, frees the teacher later to engage in discussion about the quality of the work in hand, and to become attuned to the needs of the children through careful observation of their meta-linguistic communication while working on the set task. The better the task is set, therefore, the better the motivation and the less 'control' is required.

Conclusions

The relationship between aesthetic awareness, the ability to 'appreciate' art, and the ability to 'create' art, remains, still, largely unexplored, although the evidence offered in this chapter suggests that the teacher's philosophy and approach to children's education and development of understanding has a crucial role to play. Her ability to employ her own knowledge in the service of the children she teaches, at an appropriate level of discourse, instruction and organisation depends on her ability to read the verbal, graphic and meta-linguistic signs offered by children, in order to assess their levels of competence, understanding and potential. Only with such evidence can she effect appropriate 'scaffolding' and achieve 'handover'.

 Good teaching will be reflexive, sensitive to the possibility of different kinds of understanding . . . through the careful creation of context . . . if teachers insist on retaining tight control, dominating the agenda and discussion, . . . even their more successful pupils will remain 'scaffolded' . . . unable to function independently.   (Edwards and Mercer, 1987, p. 167)

As children develop oral fluency, they become aware of the status of language, and in consequence their confidence in using visual imagery declines and their output diminishes. This is the challenge with which primary teachers in particular must grapple. The culture in which we live and teach, dominated as it is by language, has brought about those uncertainties our colleagues articulate about teaching visual art. It may be helpful, even liberating, to remember that art defies description, is outside conventional forms of definition and is therefore not easily quantified or analysed. The pressure on us to define in language terms, has diminished our ability to express and communicate through visual art and to relate to and engage in the art of others.

The Kingman Report (1988) acknowledged the need to focus more on oral skills within primary teaching. The desire to improve this state of affairs, along with the concentration on assessment and evaluation requirements of Ofsted, has put increasing emphasis on children's talk. As a result, the notion of children's art as an independent and alternative form of expression and communication, is being undermined by the pressure to engage in spoken discourse, about their work and that of others.

Much, of course, depends on the teacher's confidence and communicative competence. Other factors which inform the quality, effectiveness and usefulness of discourse within art teaching are:

- the classroom context, including the established discourse strategies of the teacher within the whole school ethos;
- the ability of the teacher to match the level of both the task and the associated discourse with the current and potential levels of understanding of the pupils;
- the clarity of the teacher's thinking and ability to set a task which offers a comfortable starting point and sufficient challenge to enable children to engage with it with confidence and anticipation;
- the familiarity of the teacher with the 'genre' being considered;
- the security of the teacher in the value of the discipline as well as the particular aspect of it being taught;
- the ability of the teacher to discriminate between the type of order which typifies good studio practice and the chaos which usually precedes the emergence of a worthwhile creative product.

What the authors observe in the artwork and art working of children supports the view that their art affords valuable opportunities to explore, represent and interpret a range of ideas with a rich visual vocabulary, for which language would be an inadequate alternative.

Notes

1 Artists and/or works of art referred to in this chapter can be found in *The Art Book* (1994, Phaidon).
2 Marie Braquemond: Impressionist painter, not included in *The Art Book*.

References

BARNES, D. (1976) *From Communication to Curriculum*, London: Penguin.

BARNES, D. and SHEERAN, Y. (1992) 'Oracy and genre: speech styles in the classroom', in NORMAN, J. (ed.) *Thinking Voices: The Work of the National Oracy Project*, London: Hodder and Stoughton, pp. 90–9.

Bruner, J. S. (1983) *In Search of Mind: Essays in Autobiography*, New York: Harper and Row.

Clement, R. and Jones, H. (1996) *Edge to Edge: Continuity in Teaching Art and Design from Key Stage 2 to Key Stage 3*, Plymouth: University of Plymouth Faculty of Arts and Education.

Calouste-Gulbenkian Foundation (1982) *The Arts in Schools: Principles, Practice and Provision*, London: Calouste-Gulbenkian Foundation.

Cockroft, W. H. (1982) *Mathematics Counts: Report of the Committee of Inquiry into the Teaching of Mathematics in Schools*, London: HMSO.

Edwards, D. and Mercer, N. (1987) *Common Knowledge*, London: Routledge.

Eke, R. and Croll, P. (1992) 'Television formats and children's classifications of their viewing', in *Journal of Educational Television* **18**, nos 2–9.

Forrestal, P. (1992) 'Structuring the learning experience', in Norman, J. (ed.) *Thinking Voices: The Work of the National Oracy Project*, London: Hodder and Stoughton, pp. 156–66.

Gardner, H. (1980) *Artful Scribbles,* London: Jill Norman.

Holt, D. (1989) 'Grasping the nettle: the arts in the primary school', in Ross, M. (ed.) *The Claims of Feeling: Readings in Aesthetic Education*, London: Falmer Press, pp. 142–63.

Kelly, G. A. (1963) *The Theory of Personality: The Psychology of Personal Constructs*, New York: Norton.

Kingman, J. (1988) *Report of the Committee of Inquiry into the Teaching of English Language*, London: HMSO.

Norman, J. (ed.) (1992) *Thinking Voices: The Work of the National Oracy Project*, London: Hodder and Stoughton.

Osbourn, R. (1989) 'Exploring aesthetic appraisal: repertory grid technique', in Ross, M. (ed.) *The Claims of Feeling: Readings in Aesthetic Education*, London: Falmer, pp. 312–41.

Plowden Report (1967) *Children and Their Primary Schools: A Report of the Central Advisory Council for Education*, London: HMSO.

Qualifications and Curriculum Authority (1998) *Maintaining Breadth and Balance at Key Stages 1 and 2*, London: QCA.

Tickle, L. (1996) *Understanding Art in Primary Schools: Cases from Teachers' Research*, London: Routledge.

Further reading

NORMAN, J. (ed.) (1992) *Thinking Voices: The Work of the National Oracy Project*, London: Hodder and Stoughton.
This very accessible text celebrates the centrality of talk in the primary classroom, through an examination of issues by classroom teachers as well as well known authorities in the field of oracy. It is both instructive and thought-provoking.

EDWARDS, D. and MERCER, N. (1987) *Common Knowledge*, London: Routledge.
This detailed examination of classroom communication is presented as a creation of 'common knowledge' or shared understanding between pupil and teacher. It is about the ways in which knowledge is treated in the classroom, and sheds light on how relevant, productive talk contributes to the learning process.

PHAIDON PRESS (1994) *The Art Book*, London: Phaidon.
This ia an A–Z guide of 500 great (mostly Western) painters and sculptors, from medieval to modern times. There are biographical details, and a high-quality full-colour plate of a typical work of each artist, with explanatory information, and useful cross-referenced glossaries of artistic movements and technical terms. Available in lavish hardback, a welcome addition to any school library, or very inexpensive paperback, it is highly recommended as a reference text to anyone concerned with primary art education. It does not pretend to be universally comprehensive, but it is nonetheless a treat to browse for anyone remotely interested in the visual arts.

TICKLE, L. (1996) *Understanding Art in Primary Schools: Cases from Teachers' Research*, London: Routledge.
The twin aspects of studying and making art are examined through a series of reports on classroom based action research which offer models of working and reflecting on practice in and through art in the primary school.

Chapter 5 The role of dance education in cultural development

Nick Clough and Jane Tarr

Introduction

In this chapter our main focus is on the role of dance education in the primary school. The arguments presented will seek to clarify what is meant by the term 'cultural development'. This is an important term to understand because schools have a statutory responsibility to 'promote the cultural development of pupils at school and of society' (DfEE, 1988, Section 1). Consequently Office for Standards in Education (Ofsted) inspection teams in schools are required to comment on the opportunities provided for pupils to 'participate in and appreciate cultural traditions'. Whilst there are opportunities within all curriculum subjects to promote cultural development, dance education provides an immediate and accessible medium for the processes of participation and appreciation of the wide range of traditional cultural (dance) forms.

Enquiry task 1

Imagine that you have been asked to organise a country dance class in a primary school. This is a complex process and involves more than the transference of information about dance steps and practice of these. We would suggest that the following questions would begin to extend your involvement as a teacher at a deeper level.

- What kind of learning might occur in this country dance session? In what way do you think this learning is *cultural*?
- What would be your sources of knowledge for leading this session?
- What will be most important: the process of learning the dance or the performance of it?
- How could you engage children's creativity during the session?
- How will the activity relate to the broad National Curriculum requirements?
- How do you think the children will talk about this session, with each other and when they get home?

For the purposes of developing the argument in this chapter we have chosen to draw on the work of a professional dancer in a primary school. He was engaged to prepare a class of Year 6 children for their dance performance in a local community festival, the St Paul's Afrikan-Caribbean Carnival, an annual cultural event for the communities living in a district of central Bristol.

We began our enquiry into the work by identifying four broad questions. These were as follows:

- What subject knowledge (of dance and of culture) is required? How can this knowledge be accessed?
- To what extent is culture static or non-static?
- What is the relationship between cultural, social and personal development?
- What is the relationship between a school, the school community and a local cultural event?

An exploration of the term 'culture' is necessary to an understanding of the process of cultural development. Stenhouse noted: 'A person participates in as many cultures as the culturally different groups he mixes in' (1975:7). A primary age child belongs to many communities: a family community, a school community, a local community, perhaps a religious community, perhaps a sports or musical community. The list could be extensive. A key issue for any school is the means by which it provides opportunities for its pupils to participate at different levels in community and cultural events. Can arts events, such as the dance performances at the St Paul's Carnival, facilitate participation in and appreciation of cultural traditions?

Such questions are important for student teachers. Within initial teacher training (ITT) the focus on spiritual, moral, social and cultural development is cited as an essential curricular concern in the DfEE standards for qualified teacher status (DfEE 1998, Annex A).

The enquiry process

Our own enquiry involved asking questions of a headteacher, teachers, a visiting artiste/dancer, pupils and parents about their understandings of children's involvement in a local community festival. We also observed a dance session in a primary school. We chose to direct the questions in the first instance to aspects of the dance activity itself rather than the more complex concept of culture and cultural development. We were seeking to draw some conclusions about the process of cultural development and about the implications for the design of the school curriculum.

The instrument for uncovering understandings and meanings was a series of direct questions of those involved, including a dance teacher, Rubba, who had been brought in to prepare pupils for the dance presentation (in procession and on stage) at the Afrikan-Caribbean Carnival held in St Pauls, Bristol. Our principal questions were as follows:

- What do you think pupils learn when they work with the dance teacher Rubba?
- Where does the dance teacher's understanding and knowledge come from?
- In what ways is what he teaches important ?
- What is the St Paul's Carnival about? What does it mean to you?
- How would you like to participate yourself?
- What kind of arts event would you like to be part of?

In asking these questions, the expectation was that respondents would give varying accounts because of their different perceptions and different levels of involvement. It is these differences which are of interest, particularly in relation to coming to an understanding of cultural development.

Before discussing the main findings it is interesting to comment on the children's responses to a drawing that one of them had made during the interview (see Figure 5.1).

What many would think was a representation of the Chinese concepts of the balance of Yin and Yan, two children interpreted freely and with clear personal commitment, as a symbol of martial arts and as a portrayal of black, white and mixed race. Rubba, the visiting professional dancer, expressed surprise at this, himself understanding this same design to represent an idea among the Yoruba people (West Africa) of the interlocking of past and present. It is interesting that a similar image was featured in a mural in one of the streets that the carnival procession later passed.

This discussion began to raise important questions about involvement in arts events. To what extent does the exploration of traditional dance movements, and the creation of a new dance to Soca style (Caribbean) music, allow individuals and groups to express themselves and to make new meanings? This is one focus for this chapter: the tension and relationship between old and new forms of dance.

FIG 5.1

At the same time questions are raised about the status of the subject knowledge related to the process. Who holds the knowledge and what are the origins of this knowledge? Is it fixed or transient? Is it accessible in libraries or is it partly accessible only through the communities themselves? What is correct and what is wrong? What are the implications for teachers concerned for the cultural development of pupils at school and in society?

There is a further question too about the process of enquiring into pupils' learning in the creation of such a dance. Although it is relatively easy to gauge and judge the surface level of skills in dance, the process of evaluating cultural development that results is more challenging. How can the teacher make assessments of pupils' involvement in and meaning-making through dance, so to ensure the relevance of the activity to the pupils' experience?

Subject knowledge, understanding and curricular justice

The compere on stage at the St Paul's festival did a short demonstration of basic dance skills, emphasising the *whine*, a gyration of hips and waist, and then announced to the assembled audience: 'Their teachers could not do that! How could they teach it?'

The question of the primary school teacher's subject knowledge and understanding in some curriculum areas, in particular the core subjects, is carefully monitored at the point of entry into the profession. However, knowledge of dance moves appropriate for a carnival is a different matter.

In the schools, knowledge about the source of Rubba's information was vague and inconsistent. The pupils themselves had the strongest understanding of where the dance moves came from. They suggested that Rubba went back and forth from the Caribbean learning dances on each of his visits. The teachers did know how he learnt his material and guessed that he learnt his movements with his friends in the clubs. Some parents were themselves already familiar with the style of movement and claimed that their children, like themselves, had previous experience and knowledge. They expected that this knowledge would be developed further through information about the historical and contemporary context within which this dance form had developed. The school was facing difficulties in incorporating this curricular strand in a curriculum that was already overloaded with other requirements.

Rubba's own account of his learning of dance reads like a lifelong journey of deep commitment to exploring and extending traditional knowledge. This learning had not been supported through his schooling in the UK. He had formal training as a professional dancer for Ekome Arts and the London based Ajido Pan African Dance Company, and more recently on a funded study visit to Zambia, Zimbabwe and Senegal. The process had started at the age of five when he recalls dancing at his grandfather's funeral in St Helens, but after moving to the UK he had eventually left school with no certificate to his name, just a reputation for his athleticism. It was only the subsequent realisation at an audition that he could learn African dance by responding to language played on the drum that gave him confidence to pursue a dance career. As he put it: 'Before this I always thought that I would have to create it myself.'

For him dance and music has become an essential part of his life. He explains:

 Dance and music is preparation for the spiritual journey – therefore a way of communicating, of developing your spirit towards opening yourself, preparing yourself for your journey, because death is not death, it is a journey. That is the whole foundation behind my work. It is what keeps you wanting to make sure that it is understood correctly and taught as correctly as possible.

The drum talks to you and you obey and when I have done that I feel complete. . . . It is one way of feeling complete. Because when a music is talking to

you there is nothing more beautiful. . . . Ghana is the only place where the drums talk to you in so many forms . . . there is nowhere I know where the music is so precise and so meaningful to the people.

The dance lesson we observed included participation by children in movements which had their origins in *Kpanlogo*, *Kpatcha* and *Ghahu* dances adapted to communicate a particular theme (the bee-sting and butterfly movements of Mohammed Ali) and presented to Soca music from the Caribbean which is usually associated with waist movements (whining).

In this way the skipping rope movement which had been developed had its origin in the Yoruba dance *Ghahu* and the punching movements from left to right were developed from the popular highlife dance *Kpanlogo* from Accra in Ghana. Some pupils were able to make links with these movements to dances within their own experience, in particular Jungle and Hip Hop. Another pupil clearly distinguished between the dances taught and music that he preferred performing to, namely Soul, Sizzler and Ragga. The music used was a Ska song entitled 'Who let the dog out?'

It was clear that Rubba's teaching approach was consistent with social-constructivist models in that he was skilled in drawing on the children's existing knowledge and incorporating this into the dance. Interestingly, he did not see this process of modification as a threat to the traditional knowledge forms. In fact it was synonymous with the tradition of African music and dance. As one writer has put it:

 African musicians create in a balance through which they draw upon the depth of a tradition while they revitalise it and adapt it to new situations.

(Chernoff, 1979, p. 65)

For one boy the lesson represented a particular kind of new learning. He described how the lessons had taught him about relaxing his body in a different way. He was one who took the movements and taught them to his mother whose practical experience was only in Asian dance which she learnt from watching videos. She said:

 His sister has been really interested. I've been watching him and I've learnt a few of the steps you know. If there is a step which he is not getting right then he is showing how it is and I am dancing along with him.

This comment from a parent about the process of acquiring such knowledge and understanding of dance was reflected in what other children said about their dance experience at home. One group of children described how the moves (or versions of them) which Rubba had been teaching them were already partly familiar to them from their experience at parties, at community dance workshops and from what their older brothers and sisters had taught them. These children valued other aspects of what Rubba had taught them, in particular performance skills about self-management on stage and about the responsibility of being a lead dancer that other children would follow.

Some important points had already begun to emerge from the enquiry.

- Pupils are very responsive to curriculum content which is relevant to their interests and cultural experience.
- Teachers are not always able to mediate such material themselves.
- Knowledge of relevant dance forms is accessible, though schools need to draw on those who are themselves knowledgeable.
- Traditional knowledge of dance/music does not result necessarily in a non-creative approach to teaching.
- Access to such cultural experiences was very significant to some pupils who were able to reflect on what they had learnt in their own terms and with reference to their own lives.

This last point is significant to the argument in this chapter about the entitlement of children to a curriculum that supports their own individual cultural development. The dance workshops had drawn on the children's previous experience of dance and also encouraged individuals to develop creative skills thereby ensuring both 'participation in and appreciation of traditional cultures' (Ofsted, 1992). Cultural development requires not only subject knowledge but also an awareness of:

> ❻ [...] principles of procedure for handling cultural content in classrooms, aimed at protecting and fostering autonomous thinking and reflective discussion among pupils.
>
> (Elliot, 1998, p. 109)

The process of ensuring that there is equal opportunity for inclusion in such autonomous and reflective activity is made the more complex because of the plural nature of society and the different experiences of individual pupils within their different cultural communities. The process of promoting cultural development thus raises ethical questions for the professional teacher. Connell argues for three basic conditions to ensure what he terms 'curricular justice':

> ❻ ■ schooling should be a common experience for all and allow equal levels of participation;

■ *the interests of the least advantaged should be specifically served;*

■ *teachers should be aware of the process by which equality and inequality are historically reproduced through the social relationships of schooling.*

(Connell, 1992, pp. 138–40)

Questions about curricular justice arise when the source of such significant knowledge and understanding and an appropriate pedagogy is not easily accessible in schools. In this case those concerned are largely an Afrikan-Caribbean group of children whose cultural needs the school was concerned to support in a more coherent way.

Personal and social development through creativity and participation

We have already noted that Rubba's style of teaching facilitated the participation and creativity of children. During his teaching he was always listening to the children and observing their movements in great detail. He introduced particular moves but also took his lead from the children's own moves. He asked the children to bring their own movements to incorporate into the dance, recognising that they built their dances on movements they had seen with family and friends and on television and at public performances. He said to the pupils:

❛ *It is not just about what I can give you, it is what you can give as well.*

He asked individuals to demonstrate particular moves to the others so they could all learn them. The children commented on this during interviews:

❛ *He asks for some moves off of us and each of us has to make up our own moves and show him. Say you are doing a move he takes our ideas and he adds our ideas for everyone else . . . he says 'we'll add this to our dance' and we copy each other.*

In developing their own moves and enhancing the moves that they are learning from him, the children were adapting the dance to make meaning for themselves. This is an important element in the creative process. At the same time he was encouraging participation in a similar manner to that advocated by Holden and Clough who suggest three stages in securing children's involvement:

❛ ■ *identifying the kind of responses the teacher or school wants from its children and what ethos facilitates such responses;*

- *listening to and understanding pupil perspectives and providing appropriate opportunities for children to develop the skills, knowledge and values necessary for action competence;*
- *providing opportunities for genuine participation in school and community.*

(Holden and Clough, 1998, p. 21)

Rubba's dance teaching encouraged high levels of participation and the link to the local festival provided an opportunity for parents, friends and the local community to celebrate the achievements of the children. The quality of the children's experiences resulted from the relationship that Rubba had built with the group and also the fact that he was already a part of the local community and knew many of the children's parents and friends. These relationships were supportive and respectful. This sense of mutual respect allowed children to feel empowered, to know that their voice could be heard and that they have something of value to say. Because individuals in the group brought their own ideas and thoughts to the dance session, the creativity of each individual was incorporated within the whole. This collaborative form of creativity is powerful and is arguably crucial to the evolution of culture, of cultural expression and cultural understanding.

There is nothing new in this. The process of choreography in African dance is one of constant development. Moves are built from known traditions and are developed and changed by the performers within the social context in which they occur. This ensures that every dance is new, different, dynamic and relevant to participants and audience. Discussion with the children demonstrated that they were beginning to understand this as an historical process. They said that Rubba had explained to them about certain back movements being of African origin and other similar movements being of Caribbean origin. Musicians playing Ewe drums from Ghana and *mbiras* from the Shona people in Zimbabwe commonly recognise the ancestral roots of their musical traditions (Chernoff, 1979; Berliner, 1981). It was significant to their participation in the St Paul's Carnival that the children began to see this as a long, ongoing cultural process.

A common understanding across different cultural communities in African societies is that 'we are people through other people' expressed in Shona language as '*hunhu*' and the Zulu language as '*ubuntu*'. The concept of belonging to a culture and of building one's cultural identity must also acknowledge the tension between the self and the collective. Both aspects require a balanced level of attention. The children's creation with Rubba of a new dance reflected both individual and social development, both individual and collective creativity. This balancing process is seen as central to the process of cultural development and has been identified to us by a Shona musician as 'an essential ingredient of being human – the simultaneous development of personal and social identities'.

This notion can also be found in literature about Afrikan-Caribbean culture. For example, Rex Nettleford writes about the experience of Jamaican dance, and states that:

 The Jamaican will conceive, understand and appreciate his [sic] dance, drama, painting and music primarily through the structure and specificity of his own endeavours. The essence of dance in Jamaica must come out of a genuine desire and a developed capacity to give form to our experience.

(Nettleford, 1969, p. 32)

Dance teaching of this nature brings young people to a deeper cultural understanding. Through both sharing specific traditional knowledge and being encouraged to create new forms themselves, young people are given the capacity to 'remake their world' (Connell, 1992, p. 142).

The ability of the children to create collaboratively was further demonstrated during our interviews. One child burst into a song and was joined in the refrain by another child sitting next to her. They moved together as they sang. The first child said that she had just made the song up, that the other girl could join in and that was what they often did. It was an expression of collective creativity, of unity which Rubba referred to:

I know when it is happening, it is when I see unity in movements. Unity in movements means unity in thoughts. You know that African movement and dance is about unifying the dancer with the music.

One aspect of this creative process that some teachers in the UK might have found disturbing was the competitive nature of the whole venture. The children were determined that their own dance would be the most successful in the procession and on the stage. Some parents commented that the dance movements had been kept secret from them and would only be revealed on the carnival day. This spirit of competition is common in African and Afrikan-Caribbean music and dance events. It is a further stimulus to the development of cultural expression and serves to enhance the involvement of participants.

This discussion has shown how an exploration of traditional dance movements allowed individuals and the group to express themselves through a medium that was relevant to their everyday lives. The tension between old and new, between traditional and contemporary, had stimulated some profound learning. An evaluation of the process requires more than a study of the children's movements on stage at the community event. It was only through discussion and questioning that the real nature of the cultural learning could be discerned. This points to the significance of the research task in developing an understanding of this aspect of the curriculum.

Democratic schooling: children, parents and community members

Connell's notion of a just curriculum emphasises the process of social relationships which in themselves are never static. We have already seen how this particular dance programme encouraged the development of social relationships within the school setting and that cultural development requires these relationships to build at a deeper level. This includes the creation of links between institutional structures (school, communities, festival organisation, etc.), between past and present, and between the individual and society. This also involves the relationship between the culture of school, home and wider community.

We would argue that the encouragement of equal levels of participation, a basic democratic principle, can support the cultural development of children. If there are opportunities to develop common understandings between teachers, parents and other significant community members (in this case Rubba) then the process of schooling can be a positive and beneficial one. Without this element of cohesion, the child's experiences can be confused or at best remain undeveloped. Such common understanding can begin to develop within a context of mutual trust and respect. It requires an inclusive approach in which:

 Everyone had the right to enter the house with the teacher, to be made to feel at home and not be left to press their noses at the window . . . (to be) encouraged to join the community of educated people irrespective of measured ability.

(Pring, 1995, p. 141)

The dance teaching provided by Rubba aimed to build social relationships between himself, the children and also their wider local community. Rubba, having been brought up in the local area, knew some of the children's parents and understood their cultural history perhaps more clearly than some of the teachers. Those parents who had not already met Rubba were keen to do so at the festival. It was more difficult to extend the research activity with the parents of the children involved in this programme. Gaining access to them was not easy and it was only on the day of the Carnival as final preparations were being made for the procession that this was possible. It is likely that their responses were affected by the atmosphere of the event but they did express a commonly felt enthusiasm about their own children's involvement and unanimous support for the school's decision to involve itself in the festival. These are some of their comments.

 To be honest I think that what they are learning is all to do with culture. It is not just one race that they are learning about. It is good for a mixed race child to learn about different cultures.

When I heard that he was going to be in the Carnival I felt really proud of him. I am very enthusiastic about it.

I've come today to join in and be glad that she is taking part. She has been learning about how important it is to be part of the community and to take part in community events and all the different children joining in and celebrating. This raised the profile of the school and they learn more than just National Curriculum – it is so much more than just reading and writing. I think that for children to be performing and taking part it just boosts their confidence.

He has commented of how much he has to do with other people and other children so it is a way of bringing him out. I think that it is important that the children do get involved in things like this.

Two parents who knew Rubba and who had danced with him before took great interest in the new dances their daughters had learned. One mother claimed to be 'steeped in this music already through reggae beat'. She took part in the festival every year and brought her daughter along, 'even before she was born'. She displayed great enthusiasm for her daughter's participation, saying: 'We have come to see what more they have learned.'

Comments like those above alert us to new and exciting possibilities in debates about the role of parents and other community members in education. Where parents have previously been seen as partners, consumers and even problems (Docking, 1990), the experience of this initiative began to illustrate how they could, with support from skilled members of the community, be seen as *contributors* to curriculum innovation and to the wider project of meeting the challenge of social and cultural change through education.

Conclusions: dance and cultural development

At a surface level there was a clearly discernible atmosphere of great concentration and commitment during the dance lesson observed. The session was physically very demanding and yet there was no off-task activity. After one-and-a-half hours the children were sent off to get a drink and within minutes were sitting ready to learn more.

At a deeper level the enquiry has begun to reveal ways in which the learning has been significant for these children. Indications are that parents have also valued the activity highly, although, in effect, the programme has been extra-curricular, an additional and optional component. Our enquiry suggests that such arts activities can have a vital role in the cultural development of children.

The notion of culture in this chapter has been broad and reflects what Willis called 'grounded aesthetics' (1990) in that the activities described incorporated the previous knowledge and everyday experiences of the child and reflected a perception of culture as a constantly evolving process. This arts programme was a process through which cultural meanings were being developed. It was what Elliott has termed a 'dynamic process of cultural induction' as opposed to a 'passive process aimed at securing conformity' (Elliott, 1998, p. 109).

The enquiry process has revealed that the children began to be able to communicate and share their feelings and meanings. If we use the analogy described by Fennes and Hapgood (1997) that culture is like an iceberg and that visible surface features, like a dance, represent only a small part of the experience, then the provision of opportunities for children to reflect on and discuss such experiences are very important. As they put it, 'A large proportion of what constitutes culture is beyond or below conscious awareness. This does not mean that it has less influence . . .' (Fennes and Hapgood, 1997, p. 14).

It seems to us that, in this programme, cultural development occurred at two levels. At a surface level, children learnt about dance movements and about the social context within which dancers express themselves through such movements. At a deeper level, the process of creativity encouraged the children to become personally involved and to begin to construct meanings for themselves and as a group.

In short, we have seen how culture is the practice of shared meanings or shared conceptual maps. It is a process of developing meaning through the individual's engagement in community. As an expressive art form, dance is one way in which communities or social groups express meaning developed amongst themselves. The outcome of the programme has not been the preservation of cultural identities but the development of understandings about cultural forms, in this case dance movements and the potential for the individual to be involved creatively with these.

To this extent cultural development has resulted from intercultural learning that begins to meet objectives identified by Fennes and Hapgood:

- *overcoming ethnocentrism through developing consciousness that one's perception is influenced by culture and experience;*
- *acquiring the ability to empathise with other cultures through developing an openness towards the unfamiliar and the unknown;*
- *acquiring the ability to communicate across cultural boundaries;*
- *developing a means of cooperation across cultural boundaries in a multi-cultural setting.*   (Fennes and Hapgood, 1997, p. 44)

One statement from a child seemed to exemplify some of this process.

He (Rubba) goes to the Caribbean and he sees the dancers and he takes their moves and he brings them to Bristol. I would make it more hip hoppy.

It is significant that this project engaged a visiting professional dancer in the school because his work began to extend an understanding of what cultural development means. His work not only developed children's understanding of traditional forms but also developed the cultural form itself. In this way his involvement promoted the cultural development of 'pupils at school' and 'of society', in this case within the local communities. Thus his work brings to life and meets the requirements of Section 1 of the Education Reform Act (DfEE, 1988).

There are still several areas of enquiry which require further thought and consideration represented in the enquiry task below.

Enquiry task 2

How does a school engage the work of visiting dancers/artistes fairly and to greatest effect?

How does a school relate its curriculum work to the wider community?

How do these processes relate to the broad requirements of the National Curriculum?

References

BERLINER, P. (1981) *The Soul of Mbira: Music and Traditions of the Shona People of Zimbabwe*, Chicago: University of Chicago Press.

CHERNOFF, J. M. (1979) *African Rhythm and African Sensibility*, Chicago: University of Chicago Press.

CONNELL, R. W. (1992) 'Citizenship, social justice and curriculum', *International Studies in Sociology of Education* **2**(2), pp. 133–46.

CONNELL, R. W. (1993) *Schools and Social Justice*, Toronto: Our Schools, Our Selves Foundation.

DfEE (1988) *Education Reform Act*, London: HMSO.

DfEE (1998) *Teaching: High Status, High Standards, Requirements for Courses of ITT 4/98*, London: TTA.

DOCKING, J. (1990) *Primary Schools and Parents*, London: Hodder and Stoughton.

ELLIOTT, J. (1998) *The Curriculum Experiment: Meeting the Challenge of Social Change*, Oxford: Oxford University Press.

FENNES, H. and HAPGOOD, K. (1997) *Intercultural Learning in the Classroom: Crossing Borders*, Council of Europe/London: Cassell.

HOLDEN, C. and CLOUGH, N. (1998) *Children as Citizens: Education for Participation*, London: Jessica Kingsley.

NETTLEFORD, R. (1969) *Roots and Rhythm*, London: Andre Deutsch.

Ofsted (1992) *Guidance on the Inspection of Primary Schools*, London: HMSO.

PRING, R. (1995) 'The community of educated people', *British Journal of Educational Studies* **33**(2), pp. 125–45.

STENHOUSE, L. (1975) *An Introduction to Curriculum Research and Development*, London: Heinemann Educational Books.

WILLIS, P. (1990) *Moving Culture*, London: Calouste-Gulbenkion Foundation.

Chapter 6

Arts and information and communications media

Richard Eke and Terry Taylor

In this chapter, we outline some approaches to the use of contemporary communications media in primary classrooms. Central to these ways of working is the idea that children learn to be visually literate through both studying images and creating their own media texts. In this chapter 'media texts' is used to describe a broad range of products, examples of which might be:

- a class video;
- a Web page;
- a photo-trail;
- the photo-trail converted into a book.

Enquiry task 1

Before reading further, try to think of other examples of school-based work which might be termed 'media texts'. How much reading and writing is required for each of them?

The idea that visual literacy requires reading and writing springs from earlier conceptions of visual literacy (Allen, 1994) and media literacy (Bazalgette, 1989). The commonly used phrase 'ICT literate', meaning fluent in the use of information communications technology, is one we explore in this chapter.

The case for children in primary schools using contemporary communications media has a long history. When television was black and white, and computers were huge exotic machines, some far-sighted writers were advocating practical pupil activity (Grainer, 1955). Writing some time later, an American commentator (Anderson, 1983) identified two approaches that can still be found today.

Inoculation

One approach holds that it is a good thing to engage with contemporary media in schools because we can show children the best examples, and, through their critical engagement with these examples, aim to offset aspects of the worst. This approach treats pupils' media usage as something they need to be protected from. Therefore, one of the teacher's tasks is to 'inoculate' children, so they will enjoy good media products and be safe from inappropriate material. Indeed, adults will almost certainly want to protect children as their access to a whole range of media texts expands through multi-channel satellite and cable, interactive television and the Internet. One way will be through legislation; another will be through employing a selection of these resources to promote children's learning (Department for Education and Employment, 1997).

However, inoculation is difficult to achieve. This was evident during a Dutch project (Vooijs *et al.*, 1995), which attempted to promote a critical viewing of television news through showing how the news is 'made'. The television series showed the decisions people made in the selection and editing of news. Pupils appeared to take the message that the news is carefully constructed, and this actually increased the credibility they gave to it. The result was that they became less, rather than more, critical in their viewing of news broadcasts. Inoculation is not only difficult for teachers to achieve, but it may have limited educational value. It substitutes a set of adult decisions, some of which may well need to be made, for promoting the learners' ability to make informed decisions for themselves. To become a skilled consumer, some form of multi-media literacy is required, if the child is to become an active reader of texts.

Reading and writing in contemporary media

An alternative approach, identified by Anderson (1983), prioritised pupils' active participation in reading and writing in contemporary media. This, it is argued, is justified on the grounds that it informs children's understanding of the specific content, their construction of media texts, and their skills as readers of media texts. Some writers argue that this fluency with any kind of text also develops understanding of the texts, and develops pupils' cognitive capacities (Gardner and Woolf, 1982).

This approach is premised on the active use of media, which we would argue provides an educationally worthwhile basis for the activity, with distinct intrinsic and instrumental benefits. Elliot Eisner defines what he calls the 'forms of representation' which underlie this approach:

 Forms of representation are the devices that humans use to make public conceptions that are privately held. They are the vehicles through which concepts that are visual, auditory, kinaesthetic, olfactory, gustatory and tactile are given public status. This public status might take the form of words, pictures, music, mathematics, dance and the like. (Eisner, 1982, p. 47)

A skilled approach to contemporary media sees it as a way of knowing the world, of making and sharing meaning. When the then Secretary of State highlighted such work (DES, 1983), teachers were confident in tackling it. The use of new technologies illustrates ways in which children learn by doing, through using contemporary media. The example below is quoted in a report of a 'Superhighways' research project.

Case Study 1

At Rosendale Infants School, south London, pupils used 'Photoshop', an image manipulation program, and 'HyperStudio', a multi-media authoring tool designed for use by young children. They produced an interactive programme about their school for distribution across the Internet. The children's basic literacy and confidence improved although further challenges were posed.

As pupils have gained in confidence, the teachers' scope for whole class teaching has decreased, since pupil motivation appears highest when children are encouraged to pursue their own lines of enquiry, this results in an increasing degree of differentiation, requiring individual or group responses from the teacher.

(DfEE, 1997, p. 58)

Further examples, discussed below, present some responses to issues of classroom organisation. While much about organisation for information and communications media use is tentative, one feature that stands out is the value of an adult being present. Our approach to teaching contemporary media has also been shaped by the view that Information and Communications Technologies (ICT) will play an increasingly important part in the lives of all of us in the twenty-first century. This view is also taken by policy-makers. For example, the Department for Education and Employment, indicates that 'ICT Literacy is a key skill in today's world, alongside literacy and numeracy' (1997, p. 1). The expectations of teachers are well illustrated by the DfEE report and the circular for Initial Teacher Training (DfEE, 1998).

In a nutshell, we believe that there is a proper place in the curriculum of the primary school for some form of practical work using contemporary media. For reasons we shall raise later, this can be, but does not have to be, screen-based activity. Given the amount of time most people spend with contemporary media, perhaps screen-based media should have a special place in the primary school curriculum. Perhaps the best discussion of media education in the primary school is to be found in Bazalgette (1989). She identifies the key components of media education as an understanding of:

 Media Agencies: who produces a text; roles in the production process; media institutions; economics and ideology; intentions and results.

Media Categories: different media (television, radio, cinema, etc.); forms (documentary, advertising, etc.); genres (science fiction, soap opera, etc.); other ways of categorising texts; how categorisation relates to understanding.

Media Technologies: what kinds of technologies are available to whom, how to use them; the differences they make to the production processes as well as to the final product.

Media Languages: how the media produce meanings; codes and conventions; narrative structures.

Media Audiences: how audiences are identified, constructed, addressed and reached; how audiences find, choose, consume and respond to texts.

Media Representations: the relationship between media texts and actual places, people, events, ideas; stereotyping and its consequences.

(Bazalgette, 1989, p. 20)

These categories may well provide useful reference-points for you as you read the remainder of this chapter.

Children as consumers of information and communications media

---

Enquiry task 2

Think about how many times you used a screen this week, and what for. What kind of screen was it, for how long did you use it, and how often was the usage shared?

The visit to the cinema, watching a video at home, or writing a report on a word-processor are all examples of a variety of uses. Record your responses on a matrix like the one below.

nature of activity e.g. *cinema*	what kind of screen	how long	purpose	private/shared

---

Look across and down the matrix. What patterns can you identify? Now ask a colleague to complete their own matrix. How does your screen usage compare with theirs? Consider the range of media and purposes. Discuss whether you can identify any key issues for your subject knowledge and your teaching.

Your responses to the enquiry task above will have illustrated the diversity of your screen use. Concentrating for a moment on just television in various forms, you may have noted: watching a video you are going to use in school; watching an education current affairs programme; keeping up with a serial; watching a video based on a book. This diversity of use and purpose suggests that we use just one medium, television, in a range of different ways, both as a member of a group and as individuals. From here it is a short step to the perspective that Stuart Hall has offered in his Introduction to Morley (1986):

 The 'rational consumer in a free and perfect market', so beloved of advertisers, audience research departments and rational-choice economists alike is a myth.

(Morley, 1986, p. 8)

The idealised adult consumer, particularly of the most used medium, television, does not exist. What is true for adults is also true for children. For many years adult consumers were taken as the yardstick by which child viewers were judged. This is well illustrated by the work of Collins (1983), researching children's comprehension of television drama. One measure he employs is 'plot complexity in relation to action and motivation'. In one example, he looks for children's perceptions of the 'con-artist'. The motivation of the character shifts through different scenes, from helping an elderly couple to tricking them out of their money. On the basis of features identified by *adults* as important for understanding such plots, he came to conclusions about children's viewing, and identified age-related understandings. Such procedures may well mask how *children* think about television, because the researcher assumed an *adult* norm. While there are comprehensive accounts of children's viewing, such as that of Liebert and Sprafkin (1988), teachers may wish to reflect on the value of such accounts.

Modality judgements, genre and social context

There is evidence that children watch considerable amounts of television.

Day in, day out, 20–25 hours per week is an average rate, and heavy viewers manage a 40-hour week in front of the box. (Hodge and Tripp, 1986, p. 1)

On the other hand, some studies suggest that during hours attributed to viewing, children might be doing other things such as petting the dog, playing with lego, leaving the room and so on (Palmer, 1986). Despite confusing evidence, and questions of the validity of some studies, a number of key themes seem to arise in research about television viewing, namely: modality judgements; genre; and social context. We will deal with each of these in turn.

Modality judgements involve judgements about the reality of a text. Television news and cartoons have distinct formats and presentational features, and may be 'calibrated' against reality in different ways by viewers.

Genre is a shorthand for referring to different types of media products based on their content and format. Perhaps the most instantly recognisable are 'soaps' and 'sit-coms', although television news, usually children's least favourite programmes, and cartoons, which are regularly enjoyed, are also examples. Genre distinctions seem to be employed from the reception years onwards, for example reception children know that you can have pink elephants in stories or in number work but not in news (King, 1978). This judgement about genre might also be a modality judgement.

Social context refers to the context for viewing or talk about viewing. Over the years, studies have shown that instructions from a teacher, the presence of an older sibling or adult, other activities taking place, and who children are talking to, all make a difference to the sense they seem to make of their viewing.

Enquiry task 3

Ask a group of two to three children to describe a day's viewing and to identify what they particularly liked and why. You might ask for a report of what they saw, what they liked, and what they especially enjoyed.

Note whether they make modality judgements, or have any kind of classification for their viewing which indicates an appreciation of genre. Consider whether children are positioning themselves against each other in the discussion, for example who is allowed to watch what. Conversations of this kind provide snapshots of what children can say about their use of contemporary media. They are also part of the process of learning, where children become critical reviewers rather than simply media consumers.

Reflection 1

Below is a list of terms which children will learn in acquiring print literacy. Try to identify a visual equivalent for each term.

- a single word
- a sentence
- a full stop
- an exclamation mark
- a grammatically correct statement

How is a photograph of a revolver similar to the word?

A teacher would know if a sentence was properly constructed, but to what extent can the same be said of an image?

Some generalisations about children's learning about television are possible. Form and content are bound up with each other in children's learning. Children learn television formats over time, moving from attention to specific on-screen features and soundtracks, to an understanding of plots of increasing complexity (Bryant and Anderson, 1983). The format of a text is also bound up with the story it tells. Walkerdine (1987) illustrated this with the example of girls' comic strips, in which a crisis is resolved thanks to the heroine's ability to adopt a submissive or servile position.

Defining 'visual literacy'

Your responses may have highlighted strengths that new literacies bring to the classroom as well as highlighting some challenges in assuming direct parallels.

A simple activity like the one above is suggestive of the weakness of simple comparisons between 'literacies' (see also Buckingham, 1992). The response teachers make is likely to be premised on the view taken of contemporary conceptions of the 'new literacies'. Most ways of describing these new literacies are contentious. They are found in discussions of technological literacy (Lewis and Gagel, 1992), media literacy (Buckingham, 1992) and visual literacy (Allen, 1994).

One response has been to define visual literacy in terms of conventions embodied in existing works of art, that is, by learning about the works of great painters children can become visually literate. Valuable as such work is, it has its limitations as an approach to visual literacy. It over-emphasises *reading* images at the expense of *understanding how to create personal images* (see also Allen, 1994). To move towards visual literacy is to engage in the process of developing an appropriate visual form, such as a photograph, to represent personal, idiosyncratic, meanings. This process necessitates an engagement which is best understood as a dialogue between artefact and author, in that it involves expression, response, editing, and modification. Through this dialogue intentions are identified, an image is produced, the image is modified, intentions change, and the image is modified again. To engage in this dialogue, children must become familiar with the cultural, social and personal histories involved, and relate these to a wide range of visual texts. A similar position is discussed by Feldman (1997) with specific reference to teachers' knowledge. Perhaps a notion of visual literacy can best be apprehended if it is considered as a process, not a product.

Speaking, listening, reading and writing in contemporary media activities

A key feature of current research is that there are clear classroom implications of the status of talk in understanding children's media learning. In the school setting, pupil talk, teacher talk and the arrangements we make to promote learning are all closely connected. Such activities are often described as 'scaffolding' (Bruner, 1986), and we take the view that as teachers we should be scaffolding children's understanding of contemporary media forms.

Alongside teacher and pupil talk, a key aspect of scaffolding lies in the nature of the task pupils undertake. We have asserted that being ICT literate requires reading and writing media texts. In the case study discussed below, we have identified a number of key tasks which are involved in the process of producing media texts of all kinds.

Case Study 2

Two students training to be teachers undertook some work connected with a project on mini-beasts (insects), in which they scaffolded children's learning about a variety of photographic processes. Later, they were able to hand over the process of publication to the children. They worked with groups of five or six children in rotation, specifically focused on mini-beast habitats. The children drew and photographed the mini-beasts and their habitats. They produced brief factual text to accompany the images.

The class decided to set a trail around the school. It was both a photographic trail and a nature trail. They made small posters of each mini-beast and habitat and displayed these at appropriate habitats around the school. Each group provided some clues on a guide sheet they produced for each child in the class.

Whichever group had been responsible for the next item on the trail videoed the rest of the class visiting their site. Afterwards the posters were collated into a mini-beast habitat book. Reviewing the video demonstrated the pleasure the children had taken in their work, and offered an opportunity to assess both the curriculum and media learning that had taken place.

One of the children's first tasks was to create an image, they used drawings and photographic images. They could have used a digital camera or a digital copy of a photograph, perhaps a collage.

This single image was edited. This can be done in a variety of ways. The frame may be reduced and parts of the image cropped out, colours may be changed, objects may be added or removed, an enlargement may be made of a small part of the image.

The single image was also edited as part of a sequence of images, as illustrations to a narrative or as evidence of research (where snails live), in a class book. Where sequences are adjusted, or images altered, we edit the image later, or 'post production'.

Finally words and sound were used to further anchor the meaning of the image or images. The text in the big book reduces the ambiguity of the image sequence, as does sound added to a video recording, or the project title in a selected font on the digital image, for the cover. Each of these tasks can be undertaken with technologies available in schools now and makes worthwhile use of new technology.

Reflection 2

Contemporary communications tools are often available in domestic form. For this exercise, you may think about activities you have undertaken with children and/or at home for personal interest. Fill in the matrix opposite showing what activities you have undertaken with the tools listed.

The matrix could be marked to indicate personal and professional experience.

Tool	Record sequence	Edit	Post	Add additional anchorage
tape recorder OHP point and shoot camera SLR camera camcorder photocopier digital imager Paintbrush or similar software Web page authoring package				

To be able to undertake all the activities discussed here you would need to be familiar with all of the tools listed. Where your responses indicate that you are not familiar with a particular piece of technology, we hope the work discussed here will prompt you to find out more. Many of the tasks you have undertaken at home can be adapted to the tools most accessible in the school context.

We have identified four stages of image work, namely: creating an image; sequencing; editing; and adding anchorage. These are all challenging. To enable children to record an image, teachers have to be confident enough in their own skills to pass them on to the children they are working with, and confident enough in the children to avoid potential damage to the pupils or the resources. This is particularly difficult because the use of equipment often carries with it certain conventions. A simple convention might be that in one continuous shot an individual should not cross the screen from left to right and then immediately reappear on the left.

Part of our task is to encourage children to develop their own conventions as well as to have a fuller understanding of contemporary media. Often this begins with some form of image study. Equally well it can take place through sequencing or editing existing material. Usually the focus is on the single image, treating this as a building block for all subsequent activities. We should be mindful that this may not be the way children learn best although it is an approach many teachers have found successful.

Image study

Image study refers to the teacher-led study of a particular image or set of images. It is usually an introductory activity and is often undertaken as a whole class lesson. Whole class sessions offer opportunities to develop talking and listening skills as well as visual literacy, as this example illustrates.

Case Study 3

A group of Year 2 pupils made some overhead projection (OHP) transparencies of fictional characters. It was quite an easy session for the teacher to organise and resource. The advantage of using the overhead projector was that quite small drawings could be seen and discussed by a large group at the same time. The teacher needed to organise the group carefully beforehand, especially the seating arrangements for viewing the screen, and to ensure there was as little disruption as possible in setting out the room for the activity.

The children used coloured OHP felt-tipped pens to draw directly on to a blank transparency. Then, they cut the images into pieces, like a jigsaw, using scissors. The group sat around the screen, so everyone had a clear view. Each section of a particular drawing was placed on the projector, bit by bit, so the picture of the character gradually built up. The representation of the character became clearer as elements of the image were added. First came the feet. They revealed little. The bit above the knee can be, and was, confusing. It became easier to 'read' the character as the upper parts of the body, head, and identifying characteristics were placed in view, because they usually determine the identity of the character. The teachers looked for, and found, some relationships between the children's guesses and the elements of the image presented.

Reflection 3

So now we return to the classroom described above, and ask you to think carefully about what the children said as they watched the screen. What stands out most for you as you read? Think about the kinds of talk that are used, for instance questions and feedback, as well as the content, or what they are talking about.

One way of finding out how children are thinking is to record their verbal responses, transcribe the words, and read through carefully to identify connections, realisations and developments in thinking that are expressed in the utterances recorded. This is what happened during the session described above, and similar sessions, during some research the authors undertook into children's perceptions of media texts. Some parts of the transcripts are included in this chapter for you to share. They have been set out according to conventions also found in Edwards and Mercer (1987) and Buckingham (1993), because these help to render talk in a written form that is very similar to everyday usage. One difference is the use of / to mark a pause of less than two seconds and // to mark a pause of longer than two seconds.

Case Study 4

(Year 1 pupils engaged in whole class image study session)

CH:	She's a girl.
T:	She's a girl?
CH:	Yeah, and she is going to school.
T:	She's a girl and she is going to school. OK Yes?
CH:	And she got/um/a dress//a dress.
T:	Uh huh/yes.
CH:	A skirt.
T:	'cause Michael told me/.
CH:	She got a skirt on.
T:	OK/Now watch this/Watch. (T adds additional section of OHT)
CH:	A boy/A boy.
CH:	A man.
CH:	A boy.
T:	Now who is it? (T adds additional section of OHT)
CHN:	A boy/A man.
CH:	A man playing football.
T:	A man playing// What made you change your mind? Just now you told me it was a lady.

(T = teacher, CH= child, CHN = children, OHT = overhead transparency)

Consider the sudden change of mind by the pupils when an additional section of the OHP transparency is added. As teachers we are as interested in what came before and after the event as in the moment itself. One analysis of this transcript (Eke, 1997) suggests that the teacher:

■ instructs pupils to attend to the screen;
■ asks assisting questions;
■ provides feedback;
■ and manages the next speaker.

You can probably identify where this is happening during this part of the session.

The central focus of the teacher's talk is on how 'media languages' work through the organisation of people and objects within the frame. The pupils' answers respond to the same focus. They are short answers, suggesting the children are treating these as 'guess what the teacher is thinking' questions, typical when a new way of working or a new topic, is being introduced (Young, 1992). While it is arguable that such questions are not properly educational, it can be seen that they serve to focus pupil attention on the content of the lesson, and that all of the talk in this session is 'on task' for both teacher and pupil.

At a later point in the session, the following discussion took place. Consider this later section of the transcript in the same way.

Case Study 5

(Later in the same transcript)

T:	What else could I put on?
CH:	A ball shaped like an egg.
T:	A ball shaped like an egg?
CH:	Yeah.
T:	And if I put a ball shaped like an egg on/ what would they be playing then?
CH:	(above the rest) Egg football!
CHN:	Egg football.
CH:	And when they kick the egg it'll crack!
T:	It would do/ wouldn't it? It would do. Well/ that was a good joke.
CH:	It would make their shoe dirty.
T:	That was// That was a *very* good joke. And I think I'm about through with jokes like that. (. . . .)
CH:	(. . . . .) Rugby ball.

The example from the transcript indicates that the pupils are able to speculate with regard to selecting a different arrangement of objects within the frame, a comparatively sophisticated achievement. The questions that can be interpreted as 'guess what the teacher is thinking' type, are linked to more genuinely discursive questions, that draw on the areas children have been attending to.

Image study can also be designed around the use of newspaper photographs. The teacher may provide a large quantity of carefully selected photographs, or a smaller number, photocopied in advance. The materials may reflect examples of other areas of study in the classroom at the time. For such activities the pupils may work collaboratively in small groups to develop their ideas. One approach with junior children is to ask children to match headlines to images and ask them to justify their choices. What is it in the image that leads to the match? If the children are asked to sort the images into sets and record their sorting in a Venn diagram, their first sort is likely to be by content and/or personal preference. In so doing, children are encouraged to think about the different kind of uses made of photographs, to organise them into groups and to consider how text affects the interpretation of the photograph. In subsequent sorting activity children can be encouraged to consider the framing of the images, producing overlapping sets of long shot, medium shot, and close up, each set labelled with their description of the shot type.

Found images from newspapers and magazines provide one source for such work. Published materials may be similarly employed to reflect a particular curriculum focus, for example images of India, or of their area during the Victorian era, or varieties of geographical features. The way children organise the images by content can provide a useful opportunity to assess the concepts the children have developed and to identify areas for further development. Such activities enable you to discuss with children the ways in which contemporary media organise information.

We have found it important to try to get children thinking about the way the image has been framed. You will need to encourage children to talk about features such as the subject's distance from the camera, camera angle, and if the subject has been posed. Activities of this kind address issues of the content of the frame, the way it is organised, and the way the frame itself is organised. The language used, for example long shot, close up, high angle, background, foreground and so on, will support children in their own practical work.

Enquiry task 4

One source of found images is the family photograph album. Pick out a photograph you like and consider the following:

- Is it posed?
- How does the viewer know about location and who is involved?
- What is happening in the photograph?
- Can you make up an amusing story about the photograph?
- What might be happening just outside of the photograph?
- Does it rain in family photographs?
- Who do you think took the photograph?

- What sort of camera was used?
- Could you take a photograph like this?
- Who will get to see it?
- Will copies be made and circulated ?
- Do you have/have you seen similar photographs?
- How is it different from published images?

Similar activities can be undertaken with children, for example pupils working in pairs responding to each others' photographs. Care must be taken of precious family snaps and it is useful to photocopy them for classroom use.

The responses we or children make to such images provide an introduction to the key areas of media education. You may want to turn back to the areas identified by Bazalgette (1989) and consider how far you have addressed them.

Work with images may involve children working as a whole class, or in pairs for tasks and reporting back to the teacher at set times for teacher-led class discussion and task-setting. In this way children can be helped to learn to talk more confidently about the ways images are framed and organised.

This knowledge may be developed through the pupils' own practical activity. The activities outlined above encourage pupils to think about 'reading' images. Practical activities should bring that thinking to 'writing' an image. Selecting and organising the frame and content of an image are important aspects of the process. Equally important are the modifications made to the image when the result is seen, those changes made to bring it closer to the makers' intentions. Earlier we suggested some ways in which images may be edited. To arrive at a final image, some post-production modifications are often required. French theorists have called this process of making an image 'realisation' recognising that both making and modifying an image contribute to the final outcome.

Realisation: working with single images

Realisation, making and modifying an image, can involve a range of activities such as making and modifying the single image, using collections of pupil images to produce a larger text, or making video recordings. In each of these the first job is usually for children to learn to operate media technologies. Initially this may be a camera. Children only learn to use tools by handling them, but in primary schools that have lens-based equipment there is a tension between allowing pupils proper access to the materials and the cost of resources. Something that will be less expensive than a trial and error approach is therefore required.

It is a central tenet of our work that talk and activity come as a pair. In this case we have found it successful to invite children to draw the camera they will be using and to initiate discussion to draw attention to the different features they have drawn and their purposes, such as the lens, the viewfinder and the shutter release. Finally, the children might create a set of notes to accompany their drawing. The production and presentation of these are themselves an example of realisation.

We explained above why we have chosen to set out transcribed talk in a particular way. In order to discuss the talk that accompanies activity in these tasks, we need a clear approach to describing classroom talk. Mercer (1992) shows how this can be done for media texts, and Tharp and Gallimore (1988) present a framework for teaching reading. We have found it useful to employ a combination of these approaches to analyse classroom talk about imaging, although we have prioritised Tharp and Gallimore's account because of their categorisation of different kinds of teacher talk. It should be noted that Tharp and Gallimore do not present their categories as discrete but rather, 'The means of assistance are necessarily intertwined, occurring in combinations and sometimes simultaneously' (1988, p. 47). Their use of the term 'means of assistance' reminds us that teacher talk is supposed to assist pupil learning.

The means of assistance they identify include some regularly found in visual education sessions, feedback, questioning, contingency management, and instruction. Feedback takes a variety of forms, including test results, but it is more usually instaneous teacher responses during interactive teaching. Questioning may involve assessment questioning, what do the pupils know, as well as assisting questions, intended to promote thinking. Instruction in the sense used here means simply 'do this now'. Contingency management does not usually actually assist pupil learning but appears to be an essential element of teaching: it involves tasks such as nominating the next speaker. This is not a full discussion of teachers' assisting talk, although it will allow you to consider the transcripts presented here.

Enquiry task 5

Look at the extract below. The tape was made when children were drawing a video camera. Consider what means of assistance the teacher employs and how the pupil responds to this.

Case Study 6

(Year 3, small group, practical work)

T: Right/ What's that called? Thank you/ A——. That's good./ What's that called / do you know? Um? It's the lens/ Right? That bit at the front is the lens. It's where // you mustn't ever touch that bit at the front.

CH: Otherwise if it gets sticky/ you won't be able to use it. It will come out on the picture.

The means of assistance appears to be instruction associated with assisting questioning. The teacher question is what we already referred to as a 'guess what the teacher is thinking' question (Young, 1992). There is an attempt to promote the use of a particular terminology, sometimes called illocutionary take-up. All of this is followed by evidence of pupil understanding, which suggests the pupil has indeed guessed what the teacher is thinking. It is an example of pupils' learning an element of the safe use of equipment.

Practical classroom work

Where pupils do have access to practical materials, a key feature is the confidence the adults around them have in using the resources. Even if the question of learning how to use equipment (scaffolding, when the teacher is still helping the child to find out about what it can do) can be tackled before providing hands-on experience (handover, when children are able to do it unaided), we have found a variety of reasons for the use of contemporary media being unwelcome in schools. These reasons are mainly associated with cost/value of resources. In addition, even confident adults keen to scaffold pupil learning and handover to pupils face difficulties in the post-production process.

Further manipulation of the image after it has been first produced can often appear time-consuming and expensive. For example, access to a darkroom requires a space full of chemicals of the sort that must be handled with care, alongside expensive light-sensitive papers, and the use of enlargers. Of course the results that can follow can be stunning. But as one teacher of a particularly challenging Year 6 class commented: 'They have produced high quality images, that replicate those they see around them, and position them as the cool centre of attention, but now what?' Before we turn to this important question, it is worth while considering alternatives to the wet, dark, confines of the darkroom.

Editing

The key to the process is editing, that is, manipulating the content of the frame, the frame itself, and juxtaposing images to produce new meanings. The meaning of the image is modified when it is changed and put in different sequences. All of this can be done without recourse to the darkroom. Different kinds of experiment can be conducted with the single image and with sequences of images. When children modify and sequence images they can begin to appreciate the main features of understanding contemporary media, as described by Bazalgette (1989), above. In editing children can learn about all aspects of media education. Thus editing is a central activity, which can be achieved in many ways.

The photocopier is a particularly attractive tool for developing visual literacy. It provides a dry darkroom where pictures can be copied, for use in cropping or creating multiple images, for enlarging and shrinking images and for juxtaposing them. Work on 'ourselves' is a common theme for such activities: prized snaps from the family album can be juxtaposed with contemporary images and text to create collages which make new meanings.

Perhaps the most powerful tool for such work is a simple to use digital camera, but similar results can be achieved using a flatbed scanner to digitise an image. Cropping, juxtapositions, tonal changes, and masking all become available at the touch of a mouse button. We have known Year 2 children enjoy producing a class set of digitised images and sending them to another school. They have received images back from that school and both schools have returned the original images modified. Digitised images use a lot of computer 'memory' space, so storage can be a problem. The operating system needs to be able to accommodate the large chunks of information being handled.

The following transcript is from a session when a teacher and two children were working with an image. As you read it, try to identify the means of assistance the teacher uses, and make a note of any other observations.

Case Study 7

(Year 5 paired work)

T: That's it/good/OK/you got there in the end/ Now where is the tree going to go then?

Reflection 4

At what point did you realise this conversation was taking place round a computer? Notice how the teacher provides feedback, asks assisting questions and gives instructions to enable the pupils to edit the image.

CH1:	There.
CH2:	There a bit of things.
T:	Yes/we can cover these over. You want the tree there/Now that is a bit thick that paintbrush/ I don't know.What do you think?
CH1/2:	Yeeah.
T:	A bit big really isn't it? So you want to get rid of that/So undo that/Just go edit undo/Up to edit/Take the arrow up onto edit. Now pull down one to undo/that first one there.
CH2:	What did you do?

Probably the easiest method of seeing how editing makes a difference is the production of a book. In infant schools, themes such as 'people who help us', using images such as photographs, provide the subject for an enlarged text (big book). Sometimes interesting results arise unexpectedly, as when thin strips of card left over from such a book can provide the covers for tall thin books, ideal for books of tall stories. These too can be illustrated by photographs and raise some interesting challenges.

As the Rosendale work (DfEE, 1997) indicated, when children are encouraged to pursue their own lines of enquiry, this results in an increasing degree of differentiation, requiring individual or group responses from the teacher. One tall story, 'The Day Miss Brooker Shrank', required the co-operation of the Headteacher in the lead role. She found a lot of time and patience while children set up their camera angles and distance, and organised the content of the frame.

A second way of manipulating sequences of images is through the image trail, such as a trail of the places in school that the pupils want to show visitors and provides an interesting addition to parents' evenings. Junior children might learn something about selection if they make a set of images showing the places in the school they would like improved. Such work might include a record of the amount of playground space available for girls. Sometimes it could lead to a pupils' anti-litter campaign.

Activities like these always raise questions of modality judgements, judgements we make about images and reality. Discussion with children might centre around how two sets of images can give such different impressions of the same school. Which views are likely to be taken up and published? Such work develops pupils' grasp of media languages and introduces them to issues with regard to media agency, audience, technology and representation.

Perhaps the easiest sequencing activity is to use found or published images. You might ask groups of children to organise them into a story. You may need to remind the pupils of the way text is added in comics and photo-stories. Text blocks, speech-bubbles, and thought-bubbles can be useful approaches. In reviewing these texts with children you might remind them about, and make an assessment of, what they know about the construction of stories, and how this articulates with the organisation of the images.

Moving images

In some ways video is an appealing medium. Its advantages include the ease of use, the rapidity of results, and the capacity for moving images and sound. However, until the advent of cheap editing equipment, many of the editing decisions have to be made before the camera rolls. The usual process is for the children to construct a storyboard, which is a series of drawings, set out like a cartoon strip, to plan visual and auditory aspects of a film in advance. This guides pupils through their practical work, carrying information about framing, action, and duration.

The work we report below focuses on Year 5 and 6 classes, although much younger pupils have worked successfully in similar ways. Classes that have undertaken such work without storyboards may miss a number of key areas. They may be able to talk about a fairly limited range of features, most of their talk is likely to be about the organisation of the frame, but they can also discuss the operation of the equipment and express their preferences regarding the video. Pupils who have worked with a storyboard use a far wider range of talk, and with greater understanding.

The discussion in the task below shows something of this and confirms the importance of discussing children's work with them.

Case Study 8

The pupils had made a documentary about their town, which had focused on the evidence they could find regarding the history of their town. Their teacher organised a tour of the town and the children located buildings they considered of historical importance. They made drawings and took photographs. The work was collated as a large display and the children discussed their findings. They grouped themselves to work on particular buildings, and produced a storyboard for their sequence. Through whole-class discussion they finalised the storyboard to show

Reflection 5

Identify the areas for media education (see page 108) that are being discussed by the teacher and children. Compare the pupils' responses to those found in other extracts.

sequences, links and edits. A second visit was undertaken and the pupils videoed their sequences. They discussed their work with the teacher.

T: Em/ you know when you show (Names town [N.T.])/ do you think you give a particular view of (N.T.)? / Do you think/ I mean I watched it I haven't been to the town yet.

CH: Yeah we give/ We tell one part of (N.T.) but we don't the other./ We just show the tidiness of (N.T.)./ That our town's history and everything an that it's tidy/ but we don't show where most/ where on the other parts of the town it's really messy and untidy./ We just show the tidiness of the town./ We only showed one street/ that was all/ just the high street/ and there's more places where it's untidy/ and not history en/ they built new houses/ being built and everything.

CH: Yeah.

CH: Now the fields are going.

CH: New estate.

CH: Just new homes now.

CH: Yeah.

CH: We made it look like it was a nice sweet town and it was very quiet.

CHN: Yeah.

CH: But it's not/ there's lots of cars and lorries that go through.

CH: We'd didn't even say that/ em/ really/ that's what Sir said that/ We couldn't hardly get across the road 'cause it was busy/ but we didn't show that in the film.

CH: Yeah/ em/ I think in/ em / We really made it so that people could be interested in the building/ but in a way it sort of turned out/ em/ that people would come to the town and see it if they didn't/ if they saw the film not in (N.T.).

Talk as learning and for assessment

Discussion of media languages might well have arisen in practical work, but the discussion of media representation and agency indicates children can take far more from their practical work. The pupils make quite long statements that are punctuated by pauses and fillers (like 'em'), and the teacher has very little to say. These pupils have developed understandings through their practical work which they are now communicating. The pauses, fillers and repetitions in their talk all suggest that they are thinking and talking in new ways.

Structured video activity requires an enormous amount of storyboarding. You may need to provide the children with help in recording on their storyboard information about shot type, camera angle, camera movement and duration. Children might produce videos about their school for children coming to join the school, other children might enjoy creating a science fiction 'thriller'.

Discussion of the pupils' work with them is the final element of this work. This finishing activity is an essential part of the handover of ideas to pupils. In so doing it provides an assessment opportunity. You might encourage pupils to make frequent reference to the storyboard, both during the production of the work and in subsequent discussion of their learning.

Discussion with older pupils can develop a wide range of learning. In our research we found that as children talked about their short experimental activities, and their polished work, they talked about every area of media education. They had a lot to say about the organisation of the content of the frame and about storyboarding. They talked about the operation of the equipment and working as a group. They also spent some time hypothesising the responses of audiences they did not personally know. Perhaps the most infrequently discussed area was that of media categories.

The power of learning in and about media

We began by arguing that children are entitled to learn about the use of contemporary media and that the power of this learning is in the making of meaning. We have discussed this in terms of practical teaching and learning experiences, identifying a range of activities that position children as readers and writers of contemporary texts. We have made some connections with the National Curriculum, especially art, concerned with visual literacy (Section 3 of the programmes of study for Key Stages 1 and 2). We have also suggested where other areas of the National Curriculum might be visited.

An extensive illustration of connections between the National Curriculum and photography has been provided by Walton (1995), who offers a good range of practical illustrations. We feel this is important, because in our work we have found children at Level 5 demonstrating understanding in science, history and geography, as well as demonstrating powerful aspects of moral, social, and cultural understanding. In English this has been translated as transmediation, the development of more powerful understandings through recasting information into new media forms (Eke, 1997). Media Education is a powerful tool for the development of pupil understanding.

In the illustrative examples we have tried to show how talk and activity run hand-in-hand and attempted to illustrate the ease with which work with contemporary media can facilitate handover to children. If one activity has been prioritised, it is that of manipulation and selection in producing an anchored visual text. It is in the nuts and bolts of this reconfiguring that additional subject, social, moral, and cultural learning takes place. If one aspect of talk has been prioritised it is the finishing activity, that is, talking about what has been done and what has been learnt.

It is part of the attraction of working with children at the front of technology (for schools) that it presents new challenges about what we mean by schooling, by curriculum, and by raising standards. In the transcript extracts, we have used definitions of subject knowledge provided by Bazalgette (1989), to allow a reasonably detailed description of the content of pupil talk. We have applied the same approach to teacher talk and focused on the means of assistance (Tharp and Gallimore, 1988) teachers have employed in relation to particular areas of pupils' media learning. This kind of approach to classroom talk allows us to see where we are making a difference to pupil learning and how.

We have argued that there is more than talk to pupils' media learning and there are products that can be assessed. It ought to be possible to look at the images and see for ourselves the learning that has taken place. This is likely to be a demanding process for which there are no set rules. One solution is to ask a series of questions about the image. This may be undertaken by the teacher as critic, or you may prefer to discuss these questions with the children. A simple list for a single image might include:

- What materials are used?
- What shapes are used within the image, for example rectangular and linear forms and organic forms?
- What use is made of text in a still image, and its positioning in relation to other elements of the image?
- How are elements of the image linked and arranged in space?
- What use is made of original source materials, and how have these been modified and manipulated?
- Have a variety of materials and production methods been employed?
- Have the makers of this image disturbed the possibility of a simple reading?

Although the image-making might have resulted from a teacher-directed activity, has experimentation taken place, and have the makers found an appropriate visual form for ideas? The judgements pupils and their teachers make about pupils' images indicate both the achievements of the children and areas of understanding that might be developed.

In this chapter we have taken the view that visual literacy is an essential feature of information and communications technology literacy. Detailed examination of this idea was sustained by the components of media education identified by Bazalgette (1989). In common with Chapter 4, we have seen teacher–pupil interaction as an essential element of the process of becoming visually literate and have presented a way of examining this. The building blocks of such literacies are not necessarily complex. We have illustrated ways in which low-cost techniques can be used to develop children's appreciation of, and power to communicate with, contemporary information and communications technologies.

References

ALLEN, D. (1994) 'Teaching visual literacy', *Journal of Art and Design Education* **13**(2), pp. 133–43.

ANDERSON, J. A. (1983) 'Television literacy and the critical viewer', in BRYANT, J. and ANDERSON, D. (eds) *Children's Understanding of Television: Research on Attention and Comprehension*, London: Academic Press.

BAZALGETTE, C. (ed.) (1989) *Primary Media Education: A Curriculum Statement*, British Film Institute/Department of Education and Science National Working Party for Primary Media Education, London: British Film Institute.

BRUNER, J. (1986) *Actual Minds, Possible Worlds*, Cambridge, MA: Harvard University Press.

BRYANT, J. and ANDERSON, D. (eds) (1983) *Children's Understanding of Television: Research on Attention and Comprehension*, London: Academic Press.

BUCKINGHAM, D. (1992) 'Media education: the limits of a discourse', *Journal of Curriculum Studies* **24**(4), pp. 297–313.

BUCKINGHAM, D. (1993) *Children Talking Television*, London: Falmer Press.

BUCKINGHAM, D. (1996) *Moving Images: Understanding Children's Emotional Responses to Television*, Manchester: Manchester University Press.

COLLINS, W. A. (1983) 'Interpretation and inference in children's television viewing', in BRYANT, J. and ANDERSON, D. (eds), *Children's Understanding of Television: Research on Attention and Comprehension*, London: Academic Press.

DEPARTMENT FOR EDUCATION AND EMPLOYMENT (DfEE) (1997) *Preparing for the Information Age: Synoptic Report of the Education Department's Superhighways Initiative*, London: DfEE and others.

DEPARTMENT FOR EDUCATION AND EMPLOYMENT (DfEE) (1998) *Circular 4/98, Teaching: High Status, High Standards: The Requirements of Initial Teacher Training*, London: DfEE.

DEPARTMENT OF EDUCATION AND SCIENCE (DES) (1983) *Popular Television and School Children*, London: HMSO.

EDWARDS, D. and MERCER, N. (1987) *Common Knowledge: The Development of Understanding in the Classroom*, London: Routledge.

EISNER, E. (1982) *Cognition and the Curriculum: A Basis for Deciding What to Teach*, London: Longman.

EKE, R. (1997) 'Supporting media learning in primary classrooms: some outcomes of a case study', *Journal of Educational Media* **23**(2/3), pp. 189–202.

FELDMAN, A. (1997) 'Varieties of wisdom in the practice of teachers', *Teaching and Teacher Education* **13**(7), pp. 757–73.

GARDNER, H. and WOLF, D. (1982) 'Waves and streams of symbolisation: notes on the development of symbolic capacities in young children', in ROGERS, D. and SLOBODA, J. (eds) *The Acquisition of Symbolic Skills*, London: Plenum Press.

GRAINER, G. (1955) *Teaching Film: A Guide to Classroom Method*, London: British Film Institute.

HODGE, R. and TRIPP, D. (1986) *Children and Television: A Semiotic Approach*, Cambridge: Polity Press.

KING, R. (1978) *All Things Bright and Beautiful? A Sociological Study of Infants' Classrooms*, Chichester: Wiley.

LEWIS, T. and GAGEL, C. (1992) 'Technological literacy: a critical analysis', *Curriculum Studies* **24**(2), pp. 117–38.

LIEBERT, R. M. and SPRAFKIN, J. (1988) *The Early Window: Effects of Television on Children and Youth* (3rd edn), Oxford: Pergamon Press.

MERCER, N. (1992) 'Teacher, talk, and learning about the media', in ALVARADO, M. and BOYD-BARRETT, O. (eds) *Media Education: An Introduction*, London: British Film Institute.

MORLEY, D. (1986) *Family Television: Cultural Power and Domestic Leisure*, London: Comedia.

PALMER, P. (1986) *The Lively Audience: A Study of Children Around the TV Set*, London: Allen and Unwin.

THARP, R. and GALLIMORE, R. (1988) *Rousing Minds to Life*, Cambridge: Cambridge University Press.

VOOIJS, M. W., VAN DER VOORT, T. H. and HOOGEWEIJ (1995) 'Critical viewing of television news: the impact of a Dutch schools television project', *Journal of Educational Television* **21**(1), pp. 23–37.

WALKERDINE, V. (1987) 'No laughing matter: girls' comics and the preparation for adolescent sexuality', in BROUGHTON, J. (ed.) *Critical Theories of Psychological Development*, New York: Plenum.

WALTON, K. (1995) *Picture My World: Photography in Primary Education*, London: Arts Council of Great Britain.

YOUNG, R. (1992) *Critical Theory and Classroom Talk*, Clevedon: Multilingual Matters.

Further reading

BAZALGETTE, C. (ed.) (1989) *Primary Media Education: A Curriculum Statement*, British Film Institute/Department of Education and Science National Working Party for Primary Media Education, London: British Film Institute.
A clear guide to the nature of media education in primary schools. The key concepts of media education are clearly introduced and discussed. Approaches to the area are illustrated and suggested attainment targets are offered.

WALTON, K. (1995) *Picture My World: Photography in Primary Education*, London: Arts Council of Great Britain.
A host of well illustrated practical activities. All are clearly related to the National Curriculum. The work is directly related to photography although readily adaptable to other media.

Part III

Celebrating the arts for everyone

Chapter 7

Inclusive education and the arts

Jane Tarr and Gary Thomas

Recent emphasis upon inclusion as a concept in education probably rests in part on its consonance with the wider notion of inclusivity in society – a society in which each member has a stake. This new concept of inclusiveness necessarily requires a recognition of mutual obligations and expectations between the community and institutions such as schools, in such a way that these institutions are reminded of their responsibilities and public duties (Thomas, 1998a). This broadens the policy and practice of an inclusive school to encompass not only curricular and social principles but also principles and practices recognised within the local community and society at large. Arts education in schools can play a vital part in developing relationships with local communities. It is within the local community that arts events can be appreciated and where children can begin to understand the place of the arts. If they are responsive to the arts activities that their local community is involved in, schools can ensure that they provide a rich and varied arts curriculum. Schools becoming involved in local arts events, such as festivals, public concerts, dances, theatrical performances and exhibitions, offer opportunities for the inclusion of all children within the school and their local community.

An inclusive school is one where all children are accepted, every pupil is valued as part of the school community and their educational needs are able to be met within the overall framework of the school. It is important to stress that the process which 'inclusion' describes concerns a broader range of children than those with physical impairments and difficulties with learning at school – and a broader range of school practices. Whilst the term 'functional integration' concerned itself with 'special educational needs', inclusion encompasses those who are put at a disadvantage at school for any number of reasons (Slee, 1996; Troyna and Vincent, 1996; Thomas, Walker and Webb, 1998). It is important to recognise that this wider meaning for inclusive education, which emphasises the comprehensiveness of schools, is concerned with educational equity and quality educational provision for all students.

Inclusion is about social justice, and one view of schools is that they are engaged in the process of reducing the inequalities which arise from birth or circumstance. Existing inequalities between children cannot be compensated for simply through the physical and human resources they are given at school. Inclusion is more concerned with having opportunities to do the same as other children and being involved in the same educational processes. Social justice and the reduction of inequality is thus more than providing money and better resources: 'it is about providing the chance to share in the common wealth of the mainstream school and its culture' (Thomas, 1998, p. 9).

When related to the role of arts education in schools, this debate throws up some exciting challenges. Here, 'the arts' is used as a generic term to encompass visual art, music, dance, creative writing and drama (Abbs, 1987). The arts in schools celebrate diversity. They teach that there are many ways of seeing and interpreting our world and that people can look at the world from many different perspectives. Through a rich and varied arts education, students can discover common perceptions and interpretations and learn to celebrate similarities and differences between each other. Children learning together in this way can enjoy worthwhile educational experiences, educational equity and perhaps ultimately, achieve greater social justice.

The arts world

An inclusive society will empower and enable people from all cultures and communities regardless of their gender, ethnicity, age, physical or intellectual ability, to develop their perceptive and expressive skills through the arts. It is useful here to consider policy and practice in the arts world. Through its funding mechanisms the Arts Council has attempted to develop a more inclusive approach to arts activity. For instance, in its publication *Arts 4 Everyone,* there are built-in requirements (for funding bids) for a statement about equality of opportunity, and also for some form of educational activity to be included. This has further encouraged the development of working partnerships between arts organisations and educational institutions, one example being the 'education officer' posts in museums, art galleries and the like. The Arts Council has clearly stated principles about equity and the development of provision for groups of people who have not previously had a voice within the arts. The Attenborough Report (Carnegie Trust, 1985) made several recommendations for the widening of arts opportunities for disabled people. There has been a steady growth in encouraging young people, old people, disabled people, women and different ethnic groups into the public world of the arts. This process takes time but several examples can be found.

Strathcona Theatre Company, for instance, is a group of both able-bodied and disabled people who run workshops and give performances of 'self-penned and self-punned' theatre pieces. They tour the country performing for schools, colleges, day centres, hospitals and community groups. The inclusive approach of this theatre company has resulted in some outstanding material, revealing understandings about difference and elucidating ways in which all people are able to communicate and express feelings and ideas, both verbally and non-verbally.

An art exhibition at the Hayward Gallery entitled *Beyond Reason: Art and Psychosis* (1997) comprised a series of often challenging images by artistes deemed to stand outside the accepted art community. The Prinzhorn Collection started in 1920 in Heidelburg and now reflects 'the indomitable spirit of people who were undoubtedly at times very ill, but who never lost sight of their desire to express for themselves a vision that corresponded in some way to their inner needs' (Gisbourne, 1997). Recently there have been more exhibitions of this nature available for the public. These are likely to have some impact on public understanding of who is able to produce visual art.

Music in Britain over the past decade has expanded to include a range of musics from different cultural roots, and it is now commonplace to be able to hear music from different cultural groupings in provincial towns throughout Britain. The *World of Music and Dance* (WOMAD) festival has encouraged the process of inclusion through its innovative educational programme and its approach to festival planning. Diverse cultural groups represented in Britain have their music played in many different venues. People from all walks of life can, and frequently do, find success in the music business.

The arts world has expanded to include a broader range of people, and has developed its practices to be more willing and able to work with young people and other community groups, thus involving a variety of different cultures and empowering a diverse variety of people to create artworks.

understanding of both cognitive and emotional responses (Best, 1992). Several texts concerning the arts and pupils with special educational needs emphasise the importance of the arts as 'an avenue for success that is not necessarily linked to intellectual ability' (National Association for Special Educational Needs, 1992). This does not recognise the level of cognition required to be able to appreciate and create artworks and is an attitude that serves to denigrate arts education. The arts do have a therapeutic value and some children in school today are able to take advantage of the availability of art therapy, music therapy and drama therapy (Jennings, 1975). However, teachers and educationalists need to focus on the educational aspects of the arts and not confuse their work with the work of highly specialised therapists (Peter, 1996).

The arts in education provide a unique opportunity for pupils to explore ways in which to communicate what they feel. This process is vital for all children and enhances their emotional literacy. Emotional development can be further enhanced by asking children to discuss and explain the judgements they are making about materials and concepts both in appreciating artworks and in creating them themselves. During the process of creating, children make judgements about the relationships between qualities within a specific art form. These judgements form a crucial element of arts education. The emotional responses of children need to be taken seriously and encouraged further in order to enhance their understanding of art forms and to develop their criteria for the judgements they make. This is the educational aspect of aesthetic development. It involves enhancing the appreciation of artworks and developing a reflective approach to creating one's own artefacts. Many young people have difficulties expressing themselves within the school setting and experiences within the arts can be highly beneficial in allowing children to develop an emotional literacy that can be built upon throughout their school days.

Learning about the arts

Learning can also occur about the arts which involves children in exploration of how others have approached the discipline, appreciation of the art form and the specific techniques used. All children can be encouraged to appreciate the products of art form activity. Visits to art galleries, theatres, concerts and dances provide children with opportunities to build their awareness and understanding of the possible ways of exploring an art form. Visits of this nature can enhance the interest and motivation of children who might have poor concentration skills or who find the classroom environment restrictive.

A rich and varied programme of artwork appreciation, linked into the creative making process of the children, will serve to heighten their perceptive awareness. This aspect of arts education leads us to consider the role of the arts within the school community and the local community served by the school. From an understanding of the role of the arts in the cultural life of a child the teacher can begin to build learning about the arts. There are several ways in which a school teaches children about the arts. The creation of a school community requires pupils, support staff and teachers to participate together in a range of whole school activities. These often take place within the area of arts activities, from singing at morning assembly to taking part in the *Eisteddfod*, an annual arts festival in Wales.

In some cases, mainstream schools situated geographically near to special schools have begun to develop educational links and programmes working together (Jowett, Hegarty and Moses, 1988). Frequently the area in which they start their workshops is within the creative arts as this area of the curriculum welcomes and celebrates a variety of different approaches and responses to experiences. In this respect all children need to be given access to music, visual art, dance and drama as both appreciators and creators of artworks.

The skills involved in working on dramatic productions or music concerts include working together, sharing, listening to each other, taking turns, cooperation, collaboration and communication. These are the skills gained through the process of learning about music, dance or drama. They are not the actual technical skills, but the process skills that are valuable for social interaction and cultural expression. The St Paul's Festival in Bristol is an annual event for the Afrikan Caribbean community which involves local schools in designing costumes, performing dances and playing music. This activity provides an opportunity for schools to link into the community and enhance children's cultural development through the arts curriculum, as described in Chapter 5.

The third area mentioned by Eisner (1998) concerns the role of the arts within the time and culture in which it is set. The study of art forms within a specific period of time or within a specific community or culture can provide historical and cultural insight for pupils. The creation of new artefacts for the present time is also important to ensure that pupils experience the arts within their time and culture. Composing carols for Christmas, making gifts for old folk in the community, or mounting exhibitions in the local health centre are all examples of ways in which the arts can be placed within a meaningful context. This grounded approach to shopping, can be rehearsed in a safe setting through role play. Drama in education is valuable for all children but particularly for pupils experiencing difficulties, as it is 'a motivating force, capitalizing on children's play; a means for personal and social development and a teaching method' (Peter, 1994, p. 5). Role play is a useful tool for exploring a range of life skills and can be employed to aid the process of understanding others. Many pupils with particular educational needs find social interaction problematic. By wearing a mask or pretending to act out a situation, personal fears can be reduced or even dispelled and difficult issues addressed in safety. This can be a highly empowering experience for children with a low level of self-confidence and can serve to enhance their self-esteem (Jones and Palmer, 1987).

Communication skills

The ability to communicate in some form or other is important, and the arts explore a variety of modes of communication. Visual art engages one in communicating through images. Children who find writing difficult can often communicate their experiences and their understanding of events and subjects through drawing or painting. The use of a cartoon strip to encourage children to compose a story can empower a child with limited writing skills. Our world today demands a high level of visual literacy. One is constantly bombarded with visual images through the television, advertising, film and printed materials: children need to develop a critical understanding of visual images. This can be more crucial for the child for whom reading is difficult as they will glean much understanding from the imagery they experience.

Equally important is the communication made through sound. Singing and instrumental playing have been long recognised as valuable modes of communication for children within the autistic spectrum. The abstract quality of music provides the ideal medium to ensure comfortable cohesion between diverse peoples at parties, religious ceremonies, social occasions and so on. The development of language can be enhanced through singing. In fact a text exists called *Learn to Sing to Learn to Read* (Whisbey, 1981) which explores the relationship between singing and reading. Musical notation, written from left to right on the page, may have the potential to encourage the visual skills of reading in a different context.

A great deal of our communication is non-verbal, and focusing on this mode of communication can be highly effective. Through drama and dance activities one can develop better understandings of the role of gesture, mime and body language in everyday communication skills.

Emotional development

A rich and varied arts education can aid the process of becoming emotionally literate. By developing critical skills for perceiving sounds heard, images seen, movements experienced and role play, one can develop a deeper understanding of one's own emotional responses. For many young people the ability to articulate feelings is one of the most complex skills to learn. An arts education can provide support in this area and help children not only to express their feelings but also to be able to talk about them in an articulate manner. This can be really beneficial for children who are experiencing difficulties in understanding their emotional responses.

One school chose to provide a lunchtime club for drummers. The drum kit and several other drums were put out in a room for children to come and play during their lunchbreak. The children found that they enjoyed the physical exertions of drumming and it placed them in a safe environment where they were not tempted to fight with other children. This level of recognition of physical energies in young people is highly commendable and serves as an example of how music education might support the development of a level of emotional control.

Another school in an urban setting for pupils with emotional and behavioural difficulties developed the English curriculum to support the emotional needs of the pupils. Many pupils had suffered bullying and had indeed been bullies themselves. Reading the novel *A Kestrel for a Knave* (Hines, 1968) raised many issues pertinent to such young people's lives. If they are addressed in a safe environment, difficult issues can be discussed and analysed in an objective manner. Carefully chosen texts, pieces of music or artworks can serve to support the emotional development of children by encouraging them to consider difficult issues in a comfortable learning environment.

Physical development

The physical health and fitness of a child is important in relation to self-esteem and self-confidence. Many children have difficulties of coordination related to their fine motor skills and in some cases gross motor skills. Activity within dance, music, art and sometimes drama can address aspects of physical difficulty.

The process of learning to play a musical instrument can enhance the coordination of hand–eye movements and develop dexterity of hands, arms and fingers. Children frequently have difficulties with left–right alternation of movement. Through drumming or dancing, this can be explored further and practised in a non-threatening activity. The correct, right movement is not sought so specifically in dance, music or theatre: the emphasis is rather on individual physical ability. This approach and attitude towards physical or coordination difficulties can aid a child's self-esteem, but does have to be approached sensitively.

Dance also addresses the fine and gross motor skills of a developing child. It is more than just physical activity. It involves the 'integration of intellectual, emotional and intuitive aspects of a person' (Peter, 1997, p. 5). Often children who do not always find success in competitive games or gymnastics can enjoy different forms of dance. The physical exertions are not the primary concern and children will often dance with a level of enthusiasm never witnessed during a PE session. The personal and social elements of dance become more important, and yet the physical benefits can be the same.

Visual art necessarily involves manipulating mark-makers or materials which can be beneficial activities to enhance children's fine motor skills. Also the understanding of spatial location that can be developed through visual art in different contexts and three-dimensional art can be very beneficial for children who have spatial difficulties. One group of physically challenged pupils enjoyed the process of making a clay model of their school. The process involved them in much physical activity: exploring the school and making notes; carrying large bags of clay; manipulating the clay; and matching elements of space and scale as they worked together on the model. This activity illustrated a developing level of spatial and physical understanding of the environment. Modelling in three dimensions is a valuable element of visual art that contributes to children's spatial understanding.

Cognitive development

The process of creating and appreciating art involves a number of skills and concepts which are by nature thinking skills: cognitive skills. Some arts educators themselves state that arts education does not involve cognition. However, David Best argues that:

> ❛ [. . .] the kinds of feelings which are the province of the arts are given only by understanding, cognition and rationality. They are not possible for a creature incapable of such cognition. (Best, 1992, p. 7)

Arts education can be highly beneficial as a motivating and stimulating approach to development of a range of skills particularly for children with difficulties in learning. The following gives some of the cognitive skills that can be developed through a rich and varied arts education:

- organisation;
- problem solving;
- sequencing, ordering and sorting;
- critical analysis;
- planning;
- prediction;
- estimation;
- memory development;
- humour;
- concentration;
- decision making;
- flexibility;
- inventive thinking;
- imagination.

Through the challenge of creating something using specific resources, the pupil has to engage in many of the processes outlined above. Through the arts the pupil can engage in practising these cognitive skills in a stimulating and motivating manner. This may be important for a child who has failed in these areas in the past. The practical application of skills can challenge the pupil to concentrate, solve problems or make predictions, and the capacity to develop these skills may be extended.

The understanding of another symbolic system for the creation of meaning is in itself a useful cognitive process and one that is used a lot in daily life. Symbols for meaning are constantly being created as our world develops and progresses. Many children are able to decipher the symbolic patterns used in technological instruments – for example the answer machine or the video recorder, before adults. Arts activities develop these skills further through facilitating judgement-making and problem-solving in real situations.

When engaged in the creative making process, problem-solving is an important skill. It involves planning and organising materials and spaces in order to start the creation of an image, a sound or a dance. During the process of making a piece there may be ordering and sorting of ideas and materials as various decisions are made along the way. Depending on the nature of the process, the level of problem-solving that takes place can be highly developed. It may involve predicting what might happen. Reflection, integral to the process, is also an important skill that involves a level of critical analysis.

Children of all abilities can engage in the creation of artworks and will employ a number of these skills at a level of which they are capable. They can be encouraged to extend various skills where the teacher facilitates this. The process of remembering the stages they went through can be beneficial for pupils for whom retention of information is often a problem. Within new activities or contexts these skills can often be more highly developed. A child, renowned for a very limited concentration span, was given a piece of clay to model. She remained on task for forty minutes. This serves to reinforce the importance of a variety of teaching approaches and activities which can be used to motivate and stimulate children who find learning difficult when taught in a traditional way.

Conclusions

Children, regardless of gender, age, ethnicity, economic band, physical ability or learning ability, have the right to a broad and balanced education. Within that an arts education is crucial. Through a rich and varied arts education all children, regardless of their level of learning ability, can be involved in the appreciation and creation of artworks. The arts provide a flexible curriculum within which a broad range of pupils can work alongside and in collaboration with each other. They may work within the context of a whole school, links created with other schools or links with the community. The arts thrive upon the diversity of the community. High quality performances and artworks can emerge from diverse learning communities resulting in enhanced quality of provision. In a truly inclusive school the arts in education should flourish.

References

ABBS, P. (1987) *Living Powers*, London: Falmer Press.

BEST, D. (1992) *The Rationality of Feeling*, London: Falmer Press.

CARNEGIE TRUST UK (1985) *Arts and Disabled People: The Attenborough Report*, London: Bedford Square Press.

EDWARDS, R. (1996) 'Children learn faster to the sound of music', *New Scientist* **150**(2030), p. 6.

EISNER, E. (1998) 'Does experience in the Arts boost academic achievement?', *Journal of Art and Design Education* **17**(1), pp. 52–60.

GARDNER, H. (1983) *Frames of Mind*, Paladin: Granada Publications.

GISBOURNE, M. (1997) *Beyond Reason: Art and Psychosis*, Hayward Gallery exhibition notes.

GROVE, N. and PARK, K. (1996) *Odyssey Now*, London: Jessica Kingsley.

HINES, B. (1968) *A Kestrel for a Knave*, London: Joseph.

JENNINGS, S. (1975) *Creative Therapy*, London: Pitman.

JONES, T. and PALMER, K. (1987) *In Other People's Shoes: The Use of Role-play in Social and Moral Education*, Oxford: Pergamon Educational.

JOWETT, S., HEGARTY, S. and MOSES, D. (1988) *Joining Forces: A Study of Links Between Special and Mainstream Schools*, London: NFER-Nelson.

LONGHORN, F. (1988) *A Sensory Curriculum for Very Special People*, Human Horizons series, London: Souvenir Press.

MOTLUK, A. (1997) 'Can Mozart make maths add up?', *New Scientist* **153**(2073), p. 17.

NATIONAL ASSOCIATION FOR SPECIAL EDUCATIONAL NEEDS (NASEN) (1992) *The Music Curriculum and Special Educational Needs*, Stafford: NASEN Enterprises.

NEELANDS, J. (1992) *Learning through Imagined Experience*, London: Hodder & Stoughton.

PETER, M. (1994) *Drama for All*, London: David Fulton.

PETER, M. (1996) *Art for All 1: The Framework*, London: David Fulton.

PETER, M. (1997) *Making Dance Special*, London: David Fulton.

ROAF, C. and BINES, H. (eds) (1989) *Needs, Rights and Opportunities*, London: Falmer Press.

SLEE, R. (1996) 'Disability, class and poverty: school structures and policing identities', in CHRISTENSEN, C. and RIZVI, F. (eds) *Disability and the Dilemmas of Education and Justice*, Buckingham: Open University Press.

TARR, J. (1997) 'Dramatic liaisons: collaboration between special and mainstream schools', in DWYFOR DAVIES, J. and GARNER, P. (eds) *At the Crossroads: Special Educational Needs and Teacher Education*, London: David Fulton.

THOMAS, G. (1998) 'Rewarding inclusive schools (and penalising the exclusive)', *British Journal of Curriculum and Assessment*, **8**(1), pp. 21–22, 38.

THOMAS, G., WALKER, D. and WEBB, J. (1998) *The Making of the Inclusive School*, London: Routledge.

TROYNA, B. and VINCENT, C. (1996) 'The ideology of expertism: the framing of special education and racial equality policies in the local state', in CHRISTENSEN, C. and

Rizvi, F. (eds) *Disability and the Dilemmas of Education and Justice*, Buckingham: Open University Press.

Whisbey, A. (1981) *Learn to Sing to Learn to Read*, London: BBC.

Wills, P. and Peter, M. (1996) *Music for All*, London: David Fulton.

Chapter 8 Public events in school
Mary Kear and Gloria Callaway

Case Study I

The Summer Exhibition

The Royal Academy's Summer Exhibition, although unfamiliar to most of
the participants, was the inspiration for one school's own celebration of the
considerable achievements in the visual arts throughout the school, across the
curriculum and in the community. Some members of staff were sceptical, so
those in favour had to persuade them of its intrinsic worth, as a natural outcome
of the term's work. Children wrote letters, in appropriate languages, to everyone
connected to the school, inviting them to submit an example of their own art or
craft work, in any medium. The response was overwhelming, and the sheer delight
of the art and artefacts that arrived inspired the formerly less enthusiastic to
participate whole-heartedly in the event.

In recent years you may have noticed events such as this playing a more
significant role in primary school life. Nativity plays and Sports Days,
that perhaps featured annually in your own primary school years, have
developed into a varied programme of educational and social occasions.
With increasing pressure to 'sell' themselves and develop 'public relations',
schools have recognised the opportunities afforded by events like 'The
Summer Exhibition' to cultivate relationships with parents and local people,
and to convey the distinctive character, spirit and ethos of their school.

Schools present their achievements and attainments to 'the public' in many
ways, each reflecting the range and richness of what there is to communicate
and celebrate. This chapter examines how the arts feature within public

events in primary schools, and their contribution to the process of communication and celebration. Case studies of actual school events and classroom activity illustrate the exciting and worthwhile educational opportunities such events afford to both children and their teachers.

The annual programme of events in any primary school, to which 'the public', pupils' families and friends and other visitors, are invited, usually includes a combination of traditional, annual events and other occasions. These might cover curriculum evenings, meetings between teachers and parents to discuss pupils' progress, and events to demonstrate and display pupils' work and achievement.

Enquiry task 1

List the 'Public Events' that you recollect having taken part in as a child when at school yourself, and those in a school you are familiar with now. What events are common to both lists? Can you group the events in any way?

You may have noted that many of these events involved the arts in some shape or form. Perhaps some had a specific arts focus, such as a Christmas concert, an arts week or children's participation in a local carnival. In others, arts links may be less obvious, but featured in aspects of preparation and management. The following descriptions of events, taken from one school's calendar, illustrate the different sorts of events you may have listed for yourself.

Case Study 2

The September Barbecue for children, their parents and staff, aimed to celebrate the beginning of a new school year, and to provide an easy and relaxed setting for social interaction in the school building. Everyone involved, especially new members of the school community, could socialise and get to know each other better. So every aspect of planning and organisation took account of this. Much of the building was transformed as appropriate for the event: the hall was decorated and suitably lit for a disco, the playground was converted into a taverna, the staffroom a cafe and the corridor a bar. The arrangement and decoration of these areas, and additional features, like the use of background music, helped to create the necessary relaxed and informal mood.

A contrasting atmosphere was created for a mathematics curriculum evening. Pupils and their families were invited to introduce parents to aspects of the school's mathematics policy and to demonstrate classroom practice through

Reflection 1

What similarities and differences are there between these three events?

involving them together in a range of mathematics activities. The maths co-ordinator introduced the activities to everyone gathered together in the hall. Then children guided adults on a tour of the classrooms where the activities were set up to invite participation. The school environment was reorganised to suit this occasion in the arrangement of materials and information. The evening was structured to stimulate interest and encourage participation by both children and their parents in this area of the curriculum.

After-school workshops involving most of the children in the school in music, drama, dance and art activities, complemented classroom-based study and activity, to develop a drama illustrating the voyages of Odysseus. This required the conversion of a typical Victorian school hall into a theatre with auditorium and stage. A substantial audience of children and parents was accommodated to witness the re-enactment of the adventures of Odysseus, including encounters with an eight-foot Cyclops, struggles with a six-headed monster and a storm at sea, all accompanied by ambitious musical and visual effects.

In all the public events described above, the organisation and management drew on aspects of the arts in the way the teachers and children considered the *ambience, audience, performance* and *aesthetics* of each occasion. The sections below consider each of these in turn.

The ambience

Arts events generally occur in special places, often associated with entertainment and recreation, each with its own particular atmosphere. As members of an audience at an arts event we may laugh, experience excitement and exhilaration, pleasure or sadness, in response to both the event and the ambience. We may also feel challenged, shocked or offended, but this happens in a non-threatening atmosphere, where we feel relaxed and at ease. The right ambience promotes an affirmative and sympathetic response to what is communicated by artists presenting their work.

Such associations may explain why arts events are such popular occasions with a school's community. You may recall drama, dance or musical events at your own primary school attracting a full house over several performances, with parents and other visitors eager and enthusiastic to see children perform, participate and present their achievements. In our experience invitations to exhibitions of children's work, or demonstrations of their skills, are met with the same enthusiastic response: anticipation of a pleasant and entertaining experience in an agreeable atmosphere. It is the events themselves, as much as interest in particular children, that evoke this pleasurable anticipation.

Creating an appropriate ambience and environment is a vital part of preparation for public events in the primary school. Spaces are regularly adapted to become theatres, concert halls, art galleries or lecture halls, and at times clubs and museums; the school, in fact, dresses up for these occasions. Part of the transformation of these spaces is concerned not only with preparing a suitable setting and environment, but with creating an appropriate and sympathetic ambience.

The audience

Artists cultivate and nurture the relationship between themselves, their art and their audiences. Audiences are, after all, the major means of financial support for most artists working in the commercial field, but they also represent an essential part of the process of making and presenting art.

 ... the aesthetic meaning resides in the dynamic interaction between the work and those who engage in it: 'No audience – no aesthetic'. The presenting dimension of the aesthetic field is therefore an essential act of communication without which the work remains incomplete. It is the viewer, reader or listener who completes the work. (Taylor and Andrews, 1993, p. 16)

By its very definition, a public event in school is a time when members of the outside community are invited into the school community: the school opens its doors and makes public what it is doing and achieving. In whatever capacity and for whatever reason these visitors come, for an exhibition of work, a class assembly, or to cheer at sports day, they become an audience. As participants, spectators or listeners, everyone involved in school events needs to be accommodated so that they can see, hear and take part comfortably. When the audience takes the ambience for granted, it is probably a sign that it has been well considered, well prepared and is appropriate for that particular event.

The performance

The arts are about effective and affective communication, and the performance is the vehicle through which this takes place. Artists relay information and ideas to provoke and evoke responses, and the staging of the performance affects the responses of those receiving this information – the audience. Managing performance, in all branches of the arts, is an essential part of the process of making art. The physical setting, and its management, can have a crucial effect on the impact of the performance. In drama, dance and film, scenery, staging and costume act to emphasise plot, supporting characterisation and giving context to the performance. Artists other than the performers themselves are involved in the preparation of all these aspects. In a gallery or museum, the display and lighting complement the work on show, and have usually been given very careful consideration by artists. At a musical concert the arrangement of musicians, in relation to each other and to the audience, significantly affects the quality of the sound produced and the visual impact of the event.

The sympathetic management of the audience also makes a vital contribution to the success of the performance. In arts events, specific signals communicate the stages of the process, and indicate where, when and to what the audience pays attention. For example, you may have had the experience of going into an art exhibition and not knowing where to begin to look at the exhibits. You look for notices, pieces of text or visual devices like arrows, to indicate where to start and how to proceed. You probably assume that following a designated path will act to inform and support your enjoyment and understanding of the work on display. The arrangement of the display itself, perhaps a progression in the way works of art are arranged, or a chronological arrangement or groupings that reflect a common theme, also contributes significantly to the impact of the art you have come to see.

In the theatre or cinema the lowering of the lights, the raising of the curtain and the arrival on stage of musicians or actors, signal the beginning of a performance to the audience. The reverse of these procedures marks the end and the time for the audience to respond, perhaps by applauding.

The public also needs to be alerted to forthcoming public events. Publicity is an important aspect of managing performance, not only in supplying practical information but in communicating something about the nature of the event, and again artists may prepare advertisements, posters and other material.

Public events in schools are also concerned with communication. They present opportunities through which to convey aspects of the school's philosophy and school policies that reflect the community and the culture in which it is located. In their management of these events, schools draw on the arts for procedures and approaches to structuring and staging performance.

Think about the sorts of activities that needed to be accommodated and the sort of space that might be needed. Considerations include space for resources, the need to make noise, work quietly and continue with normal class routine.

What would the pros and cons be of a) groupwork and b) whole class work, in managing resources and organising the children's workspaces?

How would your current classroom layout facilitate flexible use of space?

What sort of groups would be best?
- self-selected friendship groups;
- teacher organised mixed ability groups;
- ability groups of able and less able;
- children working on different aspects.

❝ *Structure is a liberating force in any creative activity and allows a piece to be brought together as a totality for presentation.* (Tambling, 1990, p. 44)

As a small-scale event, the project could only command moderate resource provision, so materials and equipment came from that already in general school use. Finding adequate space was difficult throughout the preparation for this event and the classroom was rearranged whenever necessary to accommodate the needs of different groups.

Factors involved in planning for this event included:
- the dynamics of the class, who, several months into the academic year, were a settled group, with well developed collaborative skills;
- extending aspects of the art curriculum, e.g., working large-scale and collaboratively;
- the aim to consolidate and refine dance skills by 'working up' towards a performance;
- structuring an activity that required a more organised approach to making music, developed from initial experiences with new technology recently introduced to the class, electric keyboards with a recording facility.

Combining these areas in an integrated arts event seemed to the teacher to provide opportunities for supporting these areas of learning, in line with Tambling's view that there is a need to bridge the gap between school 'production' and the creative arts as carried on in the classroom and that 'with a small amount of organisation it is possible that an educationally sound programme of classroom work can . . . become such a 'production' (Tambling, 1990, p. 2).

The Wild Wood Assembly: The process

Most of the work was carried out in self-selected groups but the whole class together constructed masks and developed movement for the dance sequences. Discussion within groups was an integral part of the whole process, particularly at the inception of the project, when enthusiasm was at its most infectious and a wealth of ideas was generated.

❝ *This is an 'explosion' stage, when pupils are encouraged to be innovative and creative, explore opportunities, test and stretch their abilities, experiment with different media and forms of expression, capitalise on working with others. Space is left for the unexpected, for you cannot predict what will arise and develop from creative activity.* (Woods, 1994, p. 173)

Later, parameters were established, initial roles chosen, and responsibilities and preferences identified. From this a working timetable was drawn up. When ideas had emerged, been considered, selected and rejected, workable plans began to emerge and groups started specific planning for scenery, music and narrative.

From closely observing the children, and working alongside them at this stage, the teacher was able to identify and exploit enthusiasms and needs. It was then her responsibility to formalise groups, and encourage the less confident to make contributions and the more able to share their ideas. A strict timetable was important, as there was a deadline to meet, but some built-in flexibility was equally necessary, because creativity does not always follow a set path. Even for the relatively small-scale production each curriculum area involved had to be considered in turn, with the teacher articulating and defining aims and objectives.

Now we consider these in turn: art, music, drama and dance. In each area you might consider how the teacher provided inspiration and motivation, input on skills related to the use of tools and materials, manipulation of sounds or body movements respectively. She also needed to keep the children's minds on the end product, which would represent their creative endeavours, while meeting the 'brief' already discussed. The intention was to create an appropriate ambience with content that was accessible to the audience, offering a high standard of performance and a memorable aesthetic experience which affected the audience's feelings and responses.

The storyline needed to be clear and the children had to work to convey to others a narrative with which they themselves were familiar; achieving this is not as easy as it might seem. The music and dance were to be supported by costumes and scenery, in order to make the setting, the characters and the plot, clear and accessible to others. Technology was employed where appropriate, and projectors, tape recorders and electronic keyboards were used to effect.

Reflection 3

As you read each section below, consider how the artistic process discussed in the first chapter, applies to the work of these older children as much as to the work of infants. How does the story of this class production fall into the following stages: conceptualisation, preparation and planning, divergence, convergence, celebration?

Case Study

Art

In the case study above there were two major enterprises which drew on and developed the children's skills in design, technology and art; the scenery and effects, and the costumes.

Preparation for the scenery began with great enthusiasm. Techniques for mixing large quantities of paint and new skills in using large applicators such as decorator's brushes and lumps of sponge, were demonstrated and tried out. Of course the children wanted to start work on the scenery immediately, but they were persuaded into some preparatory research work. Studies of colour, texture and tone, were recorded in sketchbooks. The work of artists was explored for evidence of how composition and use of materials could create a sense of mystery, gloom and menace; how shape, form and shadow could be only implied. As work on the final piece began, the children evaluated and modified, discussion developing and consolidating ideas.

Materials already available in school were used to make the masks. Simple head-dresses were constructed that in some way changed appearance and obscured identity, while being easy and secure to wear. This was carried out by the whole class during a single session.

Music

As with the painters, the musicians and composers began by experimenting. They evaluated the range of sound-effects available on the keyboard and then explored how they could extend this repertoire with some of their own. They listened to other composers' 'atmospheric' work and considered how Debussy, Grieg and Stravinsky had created sound that could evoke place, ethos, atmosphere and action.

As work progressed and attention began to turn to performance, practical concerns arose. Should there be a conductor to indicate tempo and starting and finishing? How could complex patterns of sounds and combinations of instruments be remembered? Should a commonly understood form of notation to be adopted to address this? Further discussion debated the problems of using a tape recording of the musical accompaniment to the dance as opposed to performing it live. Would taping restrict creative and spontaneous invention and limit the aesthetic experience of the performers, or would it give a sense of security and ensure a higher level of performance?

Drama

In constructing the narrative, the emphasis was on creating word-effects to complement both dance and music. The children worked freely, recording into a tape recorder, experimenting and improvising with voice tone and level, using a variety of appropriate vocabulary alongside their own made-up words. This initial improvised stage was essential in challenging the children's rather traditional ideas about the characteristics of a narrative accompaniment. At later stages of rehearsal, dramatists and musicians worked together to develop the desired sound-effects.

Dance

Confidence in dance had grown generally in the class but individual responses to this part of the curriculum still varied. So in planning this part of the performance it was necessary to accommodate preferences and let these inspire the action. Some children danced more confidently than others and they were encouraged to create or combine movements that they felt confident with. One child declined to take part and acted subsequently as adviser for other dancers.

Preparation began as in the art, music and narrative groups, with experimenting and trying out a range of movements, body shapes, sequences, and individual/collaborative moves. Much of the main rehearsal had to take place with the musical accompaniment. While dancers waited for this to be ready they practised to other music that communicated a sense of The Wild Wood, and this helped to consolidate and refine their ideas.

As preparation for the class assembly advanced, collaborative rehearsing between groups became necessary, to share what they had already done and try out various parts together. Although not in a finished form, the music was tried out with the dance in front of the scenery. Then aspects of the performance itself were discussed. Everyone considered how best to introduce the performance, how to arrive on stage, how to signal the end of the performance, how to leave the stage, and conventions associated with acknowledging applause and taking a bow.

The use of video at this stage can be most helpful to enable children to appreciate the audience's point of view as well as to have a common viewpoint for discussion.

There has been some confusion about the nature of process and product, where the idea that focusing on process has led to a mistaken notion that product is not important. Children's ideas about performance are based on their own experience of soap operas, cartoons and film as well as live theatrical performance of plays and pantomimes and of course watching live events like the production described here. It is the teacher's role to identify and promote understanding of the function of the techniques outlined above. Chapter 6 has further explored these issues of appreciation.

It is not enough to observe that the performance was judged a success by participants and spectators alike, and enjoyed by most, despite several performers experiencing mild stage-fright. It is also necessary to consider what the teacher and children learnt from taking part.

Reflection 4

What learning do you think was involved in this experience for everyone taking part? List some general points and then some others that relate to a particular curriculum area.

Children's learning

Skills development in this case study was chiefly concerned with consolidating and extending previously acquired skills. Some of these were common to all areas of the process. There was an emphasis on the children using and further developing their range of verbal and non-verbal communication skills; reading, researching and planning extended their study skills; their ability to use problem-solving strategies became central to the success of the performance.

There were also skills specific to certain parts of the process of planning for the performance, and others that related to particular aspects of the curriculum. Many of these had been identified by the teacher at the inception of the project, as target areas for development as described earlier.

New skills and abilities were demonstrated by the children. For example, the level of visual and oral scrutiny they displayed in their critique of the images they produced and the musical and linguistic sound-effects they created. Their recognition of the importance of this sort of criticism and their interest in receiving feedback generated a new practical role, where in some cases a member of a group acted as adviser. This might involve watching dance sequences, offering advice and suggesting changes, or perhaps commenting on the effectiveness of aspects of the scenery.

It was noted that children participated more fully in group discussions and presented and justified their own ideas and decisions with greater confidence. Discussion and decision-making at times put a strain on the relationships between individuals in groups. Selecting ideas from all those suggested meant that some were rejected, and particular children found it difficult to accept their own ideas being set aside in favour of someone else's. Increasingly dispute and disagreement were resolved through negotiation, and co-operative and collaborative skills were seen to improve as a result.

Leadership in the groups became essential as preparations continued and more specific direction of the process became necessary. This meant some children learning to give instructions tactfully and others being prepared to receive them and carry them out.

There were clear parallels with the responses of children working in similar situations as described by Woods:

> First, students have received a considerable boost to their personal development. This is especially marked in relation to attitude to learning. There is enhanced disposition and skill in listening to others and being listened to.

(Woods, 1994, p. 169)

The experience of working towards a specific goal, of preparing for and giving a real performance, was also significant for the children, and emphasised the relationship between the process and the product, so crucial in the arts.

> *The performing arts have real deadlines – performances or perhaps a 'show-ing' or 'sharing' of work. There is a subtle balance to be achieved between pro-cess and product. From the teacher's viewpoint the process can be successful without the performance or 'end result' but this is not true for the children. Too often children are involved in either process (a project) or product (often the school 'production'). With National Curriculum criteria in mind teachers have less and less time for extra-curricular activities such as the school pro-duction. With the performing arts working across the curriculum, presenta-tions and performances can evolve naturally from classroom work. Without the performance there is no reality for the children and without the learning process there is no point in a project for the teacher.* (Tambling, 1990, p. 12)

The preparation and performance also seemed to generate greater self-confidence in some children, in being able to acknowledge their own particular abilities, strengths and preferences, and participate accordingly.

Finally there was learning across the curriculum demonstrated by the way the children talked, researched, calculated, made judgements, constructed hypotheses and tested them, evaluated and assessed, all evidence of complicated intellectual processing.

Enquiry task 2

Using the 1998 National Curriculum document for Key Stages 1 and 2, identify the Programmes of Study that you think have been covered. Look back at the aims and criteria for the performance and consider which you think were best met.

Teacher participation

Whilst pupil learning is our most immediate concern it is important to consider the other participants in public events: 'These events are also critical for teachers and other participants. They allow for creative expression of the self and the practical realisation of their finest ideas. This yields the most profound satisfaction, fulfilment, exhilaration even' (Woods, 1994, p. 171).

The process described in the case study was a learning experience for both teacher and children alike. She, like them, built on and developed previously acquired skills, particularly in areas of classroom management and supporting the relationships of those operating within it. This project emphasised the efficacy of careful planning, structuring and preparation. Working towards a performance scheduled for a particular date meant that work needed to progress at a steady rate with all resources and equipment to hand when required. But because the initial planning framework was structured so as to accommodate children's own ideas, it needed to be not only carefully thought through, but also flexible and adaptable, a balance not easy to achieve!

In addition, the intention of encouraging independent thinking and action by the children made it necessary for the teacher to place considerable trust in the children's ideas and abilities. This was to be a public event with all the pressures and expectations that this implies, and in planning it the teacher had developed her own ideas about form and content. The dilemma then was how much to waive this conventional reality in favour of what the children wanted to do.

 Creative work was also partly organised to reproduce conventional or orthodox reality, a process given greater priority, for different reasons, when the products were to be publicly presented. (King, 1994, p. 225)

There was also much to be learnt about the teaching strategies appropriate for the management of this type of activity. Traditional control strategies were not compatible with the atmosphere of independence and self-direction. It was an opportunity to develop, rather, a sense of working in partnership with the children, and as the activity moved on, creating its own momentum, an emphasis on facilitating and supporting.

 Classrooms should have a shared responsibility for learning: the teacher structures the session and allocates the task, but the child has responsibility for how the task is carried out and has some responsibility for his or her learning, thus reducing the dependency on the teacher. (Gipps, 1994, p. 36)

This practical and interactive situation generated noise and these noise levels needed moderating at all times. Intervention when relationships became strained was also essential for the maintenance of an atmosphere and ethos conducive to demanding work. It is a mistake to assume that creative work can operate in disorder and chaos. The experience of those working on this case study showed that practical, open-ended activities require a high level of organisation and structure, and detailed planning and preparation.

❝ *The picture is thus of classrooms with an emphasis on language and challenge rather than quiet 'busy' work . . . It is clear then, in our model of good practice, that we need to emphasise strategies for increasing levels of interaction between teachers and children and higher-order questions and statements.*

(Gipps, 1994, p. 35)

Conclusion

In this chapter we have looked at the essential role of the arts in the effective preparation and successful performance of public events in primary schools. We have also suggested that children who participate in these events benefit considerably, and that these experiences contribute to their learning across the curriculum.

In these particular case studies, it did prove difficult to contain all preparation work within standard classroom activities as a natural extension of on-going curriculum coverage, as had been intended. Nevertheless, any additional time spent was fully justified by the way that the children's personal and social skills developed as a result.

Finally, it is worth noting that public events such as those described in this chapter can generate positive attitudes towards the school and classroom. This is evidenced by the feelings of both individual and collective achievement that accompany every stage of preparation and performance, and confirmed by the responses of an appreciative audience.

References

CALOUSTE-GULBENKIAN FOUNDATION (1982) *The Arts in Schools: Principles, Practice and Provision*, London: Calouste-Gulbenkian Foundation.

GIPPS, C. (1994) 'What we know about effective primary teaching', in BOURNE, J. (ed.), *Thinking Through Primary Practice*, London: Routledge.

KING, R. (1994) 'Creativity and conventional reality', in BOURNE, J. (ed.), *Thinking Through Primary Practice*, London: Routledge.

TAMBLING, P. (1990) *Performing Arts in the Primary School*, London: Blackwell.

TAYLOR, R. and ANDREWS, G. (1993) *The Arts in the Primary School*, London: Falmer Press.

WOODS, P. (1994) 'Chances of a lifetime: exceptional educational events', in BOURNE, J. (ed.), *Thinking Through Primary Practice*, London: Routledge.

Further reading

BOURNE, J. (ed.) (1994) *Thinking Through Primary Practice*, London: Routledge.
A collection of chapters by different authors that aim to provide 'an introductory experience of contemporary research as a basis for teacher decision-making', covering a range of issues that concern teachers today. The excellent introduction by Jill Bourne gives a clear account of the background to and structure of the book. Also particularly recommended is Chapter 14, by Peter Woods, 'Chances of a lifetime: exceptional educational events' where the value and organisation of critical events in schools are discussed and analysed.

THISTLEWOOD, D. (ed.) (1989) *Critical Studies in Art and Design Education*, Harlow: Longman.
A text that offers both the theory behind critical studies and examples of good practice in teaching it. Varied perspectives from different contributing authors make for an interesting and informative read, for both specialists and those just embarking on this part of the primary art curriculum.

Notes on contributors

Gloria Callaway is currently Senior Lecturer in Primary Education at the University of the West of England, Bristol. She previously taught for many years in inner London, latterly as a junior school headteacher in Hackney. Originally trained as an art specialist, this has remained a major interest and concern in her teaching and research activities.

Nick Clough taught for many years in primary schools. He is now Principal Lecturer in the Faculty of Education at the University of the West of England, Bristol, and is currently Award Leader for the Primary Undergraduate Teacher Training Programme. His professional work has provided opportunities to work alongside artists in schools and to research the significance of music education to personal, social and cultural development.

Richard Eke taught in primary schools in inner London before moving to the Faculty of Education at the University of the West of England, Bristol, where he is a Principal Lecturer and Director of the Initial Teacher Training Programme. He has a long-standing research interest in the development of pupil understanding through the use of contemporary communications media.

Mary Kear is currently Senior Lecturer in Primary Education at the University of the West of England, Bristol. Her qualifications include a degree in Fine Art and an Art Teacher's Diploma. She has taught Art at secondary level, but most of her career has been as a primary class teacher with a special interest in and responsibilities for the arts.

Jane Tarr has worked in arts education within primary and special schools for many years, and has a particular interest in music education. She has run courses for artists and teachers working together, and is currently a Senior Lecturer in the Faculty of Education at the University of the West of England, Bristol.

Terry Taylor is a primary teacher and freelance photographer. He has worked on a range of projects involving the use of contemporary media and is currently a research officer in the Faculty of Education, University of Brighton, and artist in residence at The Lighthouse in Brighton.

Gary Thomas is Professor and Reader in Education at the University of the West of England, Bristol. He has recently published *The Making of the Inclusive School* (1998) with David Walker and Julie Webb, which documents the process of developing inclusivity.

Index